Relax,

It's Only

Uncertainty

Lead the way when the way is changing

PHILIP HODGSON AND RANDALL P. WHITE

SECOND EDITION

RELAX, IT'S ONLY UNCERTAINTY
Lead the way when the way is changing

Cover photo courtesy of Adobe Stock

Published by RPW Executive Development, Inc.

Print ISBN: 9780578713533
Ebook ISBN: 9780578672342

The last several years have seen a passing from this life by people who are important to both of us, and so we dedicate this work to each of our parents and in-laws – some living, some deceased: Winifred and Victor Hodgson, Harry and Marjorie Hill, Mildred and George White, and Heye and Darlene Harms.

Thank you for shedding light on the mysteries of youth and for being supportive as we explore the mysteries of our time.

CONTENTS

ACKNOWLEDGMENTS

Early on in this project we had the good fortune to meet and work with a number of CEOs and other senior executives who had already proven themselves more than competent when facing high levels of ambiguity and uncertainty. They gave us their time and talked freely and candidly about how they approached the situations they had faced. They helped us understand what had and had not worked and, most important, what could be learned from these experiences.

Sadly, the world at large is still more likely to punish than to praise top-level honesty about the uncertainty that executives and organizations face. For this reason, and because we gave commitments of confidentiality, we have held back from quoting anyone directly. However, if there is any wisdom and learning in this book, it is in no small measure due to the help and insight we gained from the following people and organizations:

Mac Armstrong, British Medical Association; Bob Bast, MD, MD Anderson Medical Center; Barry Clare, Boots Healthcare International; General Jack Deverell, British Army; Howard Edelstein, Thomson Financial ESG; Alf Keogh, Siemens AG; Ellen McCoy, Mobil Oil; Chris O'Donnell, Smith and Nephew; Henry Reece, Oxford University Press; Ed Smith, PricewaterhouseCoopers; Richard Smith, British Medical Journal; Andy von Eschenbach, MD, MD Anderson Medical Center.

In addition, we have benefited from working with creative and supportive colleagues. At Ashridge, Tony Cram, Narendra Laljani, Janet Smallwood, Paul Freeman, Richard Phillips, Stefan Wills, Steve Watson, David Cowley, John Higgins, Gene Horan, Jean Vanhoegaerden, Julie Gray, James Moncrieff, Jack Hardie, John Heptonstall, George Binney, Kate Charlton, Paul Pinnington, Leslie Hannah, Sue Chapman, and Tracy Bowdrey-Long all offered ideas, comments, criticism, and support. Mike Lombardo and Bob Eichinger of Lominger Limited, Inc. who were supportive in time and money as well as good ideas, have helped to make our work on ambiguity, both in this book and with the Ambiguity

Architect™, useful and accessible to others. Jerry Fulp, teacher and friend, has shared insights that are always on target. Colleagues in the Executive Development Group and Franklin & White – Bobbin Franklin, Pat Alexander, George Sweazey – have given advice, scored surveys, and tried these ideas out. Katie White, wife and partner to Randy, did the final corrections, caught our mistakes, and made right the things we had done wrong. We couldn't have achieved this without her!

Business colleagues like John Richards of Boots Ltd, Reg Hankey of Pittards plc, Peter Rogers of Independent Television Commission, George Levvy of MND, Alan Hamel of PricewaterhouseCoopers, Elmer Hakkinen of Nokia, Robert Warner and Geoff Harwood of Aukett, Sue Johnson and Martin Havelock of Oxford University Press, Peter Wilkinson of the Audit Commission, Bart Becht and Tom Corran of Reckitt Benckiser, Pat Mahanes and Rich Carpenter of Kennametal, classes at the Johnson Graduate School of Management at Cornell and the Fuqua School of Business at Duke, as well as the Institute of Management Studies in various cities around the world, have all been part of the exploration and development of our work.

Our publisher and editorial mentor Richard Stagg has been seriously generous with his time and publishing insights and has helped us to raise our writing standards beyond what we thought possible.

Finally, thanks go to our families, particularly Jane, who puts up with the rantings of Phil and the comings and goings of the 'foreigner.' Friends have watched patiently, supportively, and sometimes incredulously as we have gone around the endless circuits and bumps of coming to grips with this subject. Writers and researchers are not easy to get on with at times, and we really do appreciate the tolerance we have been shown.

To everyone, we offer our thanks.

Phil Hodgson
Randy White

PROLOGUE

Twenty years ago Phil and I wrote *Relax*. Wow, so much has changed – children grown, various important others have passed on, many consulting engagements and classes conducted, miles traveled, missed connections, fun vacations, life happens!

I struggled with the re-working of this book because Phil has moved on to pursue his passions around woodworking, restoring violins, maths, and music – in fact at last count he plays in two symphony orchestras and a couple of jazz bands! And, he and Jane are often busy helping to take care of three grandchildren as well as traveling to various parts of the world. I see them often – we travel together, and I stay in "my room" when I get to the UK several times a year.

When I asked Phil if he wanted to be part of this update, he said he was happy for me to do it. I hope I haven't taken his name in vain as in Chapter 0, I have used the plural versus the singular because I believe, based on numerous days of walking, bike riding and sharing dinners and trips with our families, he would *mostly* be in agreement with what is written in this new chapter. I apologize if I misrepresent anything Phil may or may not have said.

I would also like to thank my business partners at Executive Development Group, Drs. Sandra Shullman and Lily Kelly-Radford who have added my materials to their classes both at HEC in Paris and Doha and for various clients. They have honored me by including my materials and by being willing to co-author papers and class sessions with me. Through their helpful comments I have extended my understanding of ambiguity and the uncertainty it brings.

Lastly, to Heidi and David, I could not have done this re-boot without your help and energy.

Greensboro, NC, USA
September, 2019

CHAPTER 0

I t's the end of the world as we know it – NOT!

It seems almost quaint that many people speculated about catastrophic occurrences when all the world's computers ran out of numbers with the new millennium. Most people knew we'd survive, but even the most skeptical among them might have withdrawn a little cash prior to midnight on January 1, 2000, just in case the ATM crashed. (We did.) Most expected some inconvenience. After all, apps hadn't replaced cash at that time.

Y2K, as it was known, was a big deal until it wasn't. It was, however, a good lesson in uncertainty: it's difficult to plan for, it causes anxiety and confusion and it redefines the world in which we work.

More lessons followed.

Soon after we first published *Relax, It's Only Uncertainty* we saw commercial airliners used as weapons by terrorists. We lost friends, clients and our sense of an orderly world. Unfortunately, 9/11 precipitated a series of protracted wars that are still being fought many years later.

Rapidly evolving technology, even as a productivity tool, has done as much to amplify uncertainty as it has to save us time. We work faster with less time lag waiting for responses from coworkers and customers, and work is expanding to fill our every waking moment – do you sleep with your iPhone?

We can also process vast amounts of data at astounding speeds. How many people were concerned that shaving a few milliseconds off a routine stock trade using a more direct fiber optic connection to the stock exchange could cause a trillion-dollar stock crash? It did just that for all of 36 minutes in what is known as the 2010 Flash Crash. It was quickly rectified, but talk about uncertainty! And in response, the "Algo" traders who followed began to search for the microsecond (maybe soon nanoseconds) s competitive advantage on subsequent stock trades.

Algorithms can select our online friends, remind us that we haven't bought enough of what we usually buy, and influence elections with messages that move public opinion faster than it can be polled.

Most of us did not imagine at the beginning of the new millennium that a thing called social media would be on the front page of the world's financial media, itself causing uncertainty – not just with astoundingly unprofitable companies (using standard accounting techniques) being bought and sold for billions, but by causing nations to rethink their security and perhaps their electoral integrity.

In the now distant past the Canadian philosopher Marshall McLuhan told us the medium was the message. Today, *social* media is often the synapse that makes the message. A giant corporation can lose enormous value in shares with a single tweet from one person.

The physical map of the world hasn't changed much in the last 20 years, but the politics and alliances are shifting as we write. We now see populism and nationalism pushing back against 70 years of post-Cold War globalism and democratization. This edition of *Relax* appears in the midst of an unresolved Brexit, a still unfolding, unorthodox US presidency, China's productivity is outpacing the US, and the US seems to be retracting into isolationism not seen since the turn of the last century – all leaving a void of global leadership and anything but stability.

Nothing of this scale has happened in modern times. CNN commentator Fareed Zakaria has called it, "A time when these forces of entropy are intensifying."

From *Black Swans* to *The World is Flat* to *The Hidden Half: How the World Conceals its Secrets* and *Thinking Fast and Slow*, books are written all the time telling us how much faster and more unpredictable life is becoming; and of late how we are losing western ideals of democracy and freedom, as individuals search for answers amidst increasing uncertainty.

It turns out that the world has become more uncertain and since uncertainty breeds on itself, it's not going away.

"Twenty years ago, uncertainty meant that leaders could imagine different evolutions of their business context and reflect upon which scenario was the most plausible. It was the era of Scenario Planning. Today, uncertainty is not about probability any longer. It's about disruption that can take you off-guard," says Hervé Coyco, former president of Michelin's automotive division. "It's about things that we would consider the impossible in the past that become – all of a sudden – the possible and eventually they became the new norm."

2

Hervé knows a thing or two about "all of a sudden." A decade ago, over the course of a weekend, he went from being an engineer with a team of 60 reports to a president leading more than 60,000.

Today, Hervé is a leadership professor inspiring MBA candidates in Paris to embrace a new, non-hierarchical leadership style of exploration.

"In such a disruptive context, the leader has no clue about the solution," says Hervé. "Instead, what they need is to mobilize the collective intelligence of their organization, because *together* they are going to learn and explore. Ultimately, they will find the solution *together*. And I like this exploration model very much."

As do we. It's the logical development in leadership styles that begins with command-and-control, in which uncertainty is assumed away, and evolves through more inclusive and learning models. Twenty years on, the lessons here in *Relax* still apply.

Maybe the world as we knew it, did end in 2000, it just took a while to notice. After all, "Life can only be understood backwards; but it must be lived forwards," wrote Kierkegaard.

What's the good news?

Even though there is more uncertainty today, it's as easy to master as it was 20 years ago.

The outcomes and metrics we based the book on have been tested and validated consistently over the past two decades. We've updated parts of the narrative, but the prescription for mastering uncertainty remains as it was.

You can still navigate ambiguity to your advantage by being "motivated by mysteries," "scanning the horizon ahead" for new opportunities and by being flexible, as discussed in the chapters about our eight "Enablers." You can be first to market with a new idea. You can make up new rules in the marketplace where there are none. You can lead your organization to be more agile and always learning.

We wrote *Relax* to be instructional for high-potential or high-performing leaders. Our surveys and teaching continue to validate two facts: 1) high-performing executives tend to be better at being comfortable with ambiguity and uncertainty, and 2) this skillset can be learned, practiced, and used to competitive advantage.

Relax has served as a textbook in global executive MBA courses at elite business schools, and we've learned something else: this book can serve as a survival guide for anyone trying to navigate a quickly-evolving world. Amidst increasing uncertainty, *Relax* is an appropriate read for anyone, at any level of experience, who wants to become more confidently engaged in their work and standout within their organization.

We've continued to study and test the ideas of *Relax* and published articles in which we check in with colleagues, former students and clients around the world on how they're dealing with uncertainty. *Relax* has been woven into emerging topics in learning and development as part of the on-going global discussion of leadership.

Quick, while nobody's watching!

There can be something liberating about disruption. Relax for a minute and consider the possibilities.

If certainty, predictability and "the way it's always worked" disappear, why should we stay in our lanes? Why not challenge market assumptions? If unbound by the old conventions, couldn't we experiment more with new processes? Why not imagine the next big thing? The new, new thing?

These faint, and not so faint signals we're hearing from the workplace and the people who study it suggest that while we are reeling from ambiguity, there are some developments in organizational life that are quite positive. We'll call them trends.

Trend: Less hierarchal structure

With uncertainty comes more diffused individual authority. The all-knowing leader, or those that pretended to be, is extinct.

But relax, we've got this. Because effective leaders in a post-certainty world are able to delegate and distribute the burden of choosing ways forward – sometimes multiple ways. It's a good time to build your own leadership skills, because it's more likely you'll be called upon to use them in a more collaborative organization.

"The expert leadership model has gone out the window," says our friend Cheryl Stokes, a seasoned leadership consultant and partner at Heidrick & Struggles.

Another colleague, George Binney, based in the UK, believes the new boss isn't anything like the old boss (apologies to Pete Townshend).

"Bosses aren't much good at providing support," said George. "People keep LOOKING to their bosses to give them clear direction and clear sense of meaning and sense of values but it doesn't seem to work very often. So who do they end up relying on? In fact the people who are successful end up relying on peers."

George advises that what people need is, "really good networks of people with whom they can talk really openly about what's going on and how they can deal with it."

"Making sure that people are working together to experiment with new solutions means you cannot operate on a hierarchical structure, only," suggests Hervé. "You have to inject into the organization a little bit of chaos – potentially cross-functional teams that have the authority to explore ideas beyond the scope of the traditional business organization. For this collaborative initiatives to be effective, it is utmost critical that everyone in the organization is clear about the vision and the strategic priorities of the firm."

Thus, the new boss is you and your colleagues.

It reminds us of the ground-breaking Apple Computer "1984" television spot in which an auditorium of enslaved people, transfixed to a dystopian leader on a giant video screen is liberated by a woman who smashes the screen with a hurled hammer.

That famous commercial heralded a revolution in personal computers, but it's analogous to what happens when mass uncertainty reveals that our leaders are as momentarily clueless as we are.

Scary? A little, but think of the rewards!

"At the end of the day," says Hervé, "It's about accepting risk and accepting failure. And it requires a lot of trust between you and your people. You, because you need to trust their motivation and their discernment. Your people, because they need to trust that you will support them if their initiatives fail."

Trend: Learning is foremost

As teachers, we have a bias for this trend. Learning has always been key to leadership, but in a VUCA (Volatile, Uncertain, Chaotic, Ambiguous) environment, it's what we have to do every day. What works and what doesn't work and why are constant questions. In this trend, our leaders must be learners and nurture the same in their teams. After all, if the leader and her people can learn faster than the competition, they will ultimately win in the marketplace.

With so much disruption and change, learning must become more integral to strategy – continual learning, not just one-off classes. It's the self-directed learning of the "70" and "20" in the popular 70-20-10 leadership model that comes from challenging assignments and interaction with others.

Agility is another leadership trait that is one of the outcomes of continual learning. With new information coming at us faster every day, achieving agility is, in Cheryl's words, critical:

"We have empirical research that shows agility accelerates performance, so agility is essential for leaders and organizations. Becoming an agile learner includes being open to learning and new challenges, taking intelligent risks, and reflecting so that you actually learn from experiences both good and bad. Agility helps you spot opportunities, pivot, adapt, and address threats ahead of the competition, which leads to accelerated performance."

Individuals and organizations can now embrace a learning culture in a context that might not have occurred during a period of complacency. It's compulsory but it can be exciting and fulfilling, too.

We've yet to see "greater emphasis on learning" set anyone back.

Trend: Innovation is ubiquitous

Rapid change makes innovation both a requirement and a competitive advantage when unexpected situations can close down a business or derail your career. Being able to try and fail and reinvent quickly is a survival tool. The same dynamic can unseat a competitor or create a new space in the market.

Practicing the Enablers and avoiding the Restrainers can put you in a position to be a leader of innovation.

You can look to the youngest emerging leaders as examples. They're entering the workplace asking, "What is this 'uncertainty' of which you speak?" Because they have come of age in a world of unexpected occurrences, Millennials and Generation Z consider ambiguity and chaos the norm. (This isn't a new idea. Our original editor, Richard, had this same opinion 20 years ago.)

"Leadership today is defined by the notions of change-making and impact," says Jeremy Ghez. "Younger generations are not content with the status quo. They come with perhaps a greater ability to imagine – pragmatically – new ways forward."

A colleague of Randy's at HEC Paris, Jeremy is a professor of economics and international affairs, and is Scientific Director of the Sustainability and Social Innovation Master's program. In 2019, he published *Architects of Change*, a book that redefines leadership as shifting towards the notion of change-maker and towards the notion of impact. In his job, he sees students engaged in locally-focused projects – e.g., how we feed livestock in Africa – that have global significance and impact.

Jeremy observes a cohort of future leaders with a penchant for innovation and maybe a whiff of rebelliousness against their parents' tribe who left things in a mess.

"It's as if they're saying, 'I do not trust the previous generation, because their recklessness makes me think that I shouldn't trust them at all,' so it's time that we disrupt, it's time that we completely reinvent the whole system," says Jeremy.

"And by the way, to them, VUCA doesn't mean a thing because VUCA is the starting point of the whole thing."

Learning from youth could mark the new decade as one that is defined by people who value making a difference, curiosity, challenging convention and bringing us life-changing inventions, methods and policies.

Jeremy relays that leadership today is defined – according to the new generations – by the notions of change-making and impact.

Calling all leaders

Given these three trends, mastering uncertainty has never been so important for your health, happiness, and ability to succeed. Rather than yearn for less chaos, or a boss who tells you exactly what to do, these skills allow you to survive and thrive.

Working in uncertainty is a job we need to all share. The unknown is part-and-parcel of the modern, post-industrial definition of learning leadership. Uncertainty is one place where leaders must take their organizations and a major source of competitive advantage.

When *Relax, It's Only Uncertainty* was first published, we had been studying the effects of ambiguity and uncertainty on executives in global organizations and we had found that top performing executives shared a trait: the ability to manage – and even thrive – in ambiguity. Where others saw a dark unknown, those who were adept at dealing with uncertainty saw a clean slate where market rules were suspended, market leaders were upended and innovation could flourish.

Chapter by chapter, *Relax* is a practical field guide for business. As you read this new edition, approach it as a time-tested primer for thriving in ambiguity. If you have a career vision and are motivated by curiosity, problem solving, and learning leadership you may enjoy *Relax* as a book you read slowly, processing each chapter against your day-to-day experience.

By appealing to leaders of all experience levels, including yourself, we hope that the observations of the book can inspire actions, strategies and business plans that will help organizations thrive in a way that benefits society.

INTRODUCTION

If a man will begin with certainties, he shall end in doubts, but if he will be content to begin with doubts, he shall end in certainties.

Francis Bacon (1605) *The Advancement of Learning*

Welcome to uncertainty

What shall I do about that new venture? Those sales predictions? That business launch? How shall I handle that issue concerning my customer, my boss, or even my partner?

The chances are that as you are reading this you are carrying with you several decisions that you have been putting off, but will soon have to face. These decisions will no doubt be a mix of big and small, personal and work-oriented, and everything in between. Ask yourself this question: how confidently, really, are you facing up to these decisions and the actions that you will need to take? What's more, how certain do you feel about the outcomes? Do you have all the information that you need to make the decisions or will you have to take a chance and make a decision even though you aren't sure? How many of those decisions will lead to uncharted territory or uncomfortable and emotional discussions? How many of these issues are surrounded by uncertainty? ... Feeling relaxed and confident? ... We thought not!

Uncertainty causes stress, and it is difficult to be relaxed when you're feeling stressed. Yet this is the age of uncertainty. In this book we are going to propose that we, you and everyone else on the planet are facing rising levels of uncertainty in our lives. How can we cope? That is what this book is about, and we want to tackle this issue in a very pragmatic and practical way.

Start with behavior

We have spent the last ten years looking at which behaviors help people cope most effectively with uncertainty. Later in this book we describe specific behaviors and methods of learning those behaviors which help people cope with uncertainty. The behaviors have been known for millennia, but they have been known by a very small group of people who found themselves in leadership roles. To be an effective leader you need to make decisions, and often those decisions are in the face of a lot of uncertainty. The more uncertainty that surrounds a decision, the more the call for leadership. But people in leadership roles are frequently unprepared or unable to admit to the rest of the world the ambiguity they face and the feelings of uncertainty they feel as a result of that ambiguity. Indeed, it was often believed that for a leader to admit to being uncertain was an outright failure of their leadership.

> ... it was often believed that for a leader to admit to being uncertain was an outright failure of their leadership.

But that was then, and this is WOW! (Thanks, Tom Peters.) Now with the almost universal distribution of information via electronic networks, a proportion of the world's population has access to an enormous range of data. Suddenly all of us are aware of the uncertainties and ambiguities that face leaders. So what can we learn? The first part of this book will describe behaviors to cope effectively with increasing levels of ambiguity.

Leaders, leaders everywhere

But if I'm using leadership behaviors, doesn't that make me a leader? you may ask. Yes, of course. Everyone's a leader now. But surely there's a lot more to leadership than handling ambiguity? What about leadership style? What about the other skills of leadership that I have already learned? Are they all redundant now?

To be an effective leader in any context one of the main requirements is to assess the style and skills needed to be effective in that situation. In the second part of this book we help you calibrate your leadership style and the appropriate behavior needed to lead the way when the way is changing. We want to help you make sure that your behavior will fit the context.

The real work of leadership is embracing ambiguity

If only Woody Allen's observation were true – that "80 percent of success is [just] showing up."[1] Yet there seems to be a very narrow edge between certainty and uncertainty, success and failure. Leadership is what crosses the frontier between what we did yesterday and what we'll do tomorrow. We'll argue in this book that the real mark of a leader is confidence with uncertainty – the ability to admit to it and deal with it. And just to be clear, we think ambiguity is how it is, and uncertainty is how you feel about it. So the effective leader is always coping with his or her own feelings of uncertainty in the face of ambiguity.

As we researched this book, we uncovered a lot of evidence[2&3] showing that an enormous proportion of leadership development is done

> Ambiguity is how it is. Uncertainty is how you feel about it.

through early experience and in our everyday lives. This suggests that some of the behaviors that people use in leadership roles were not always consciously learned, but picked up along the way as they met and coped with various life experiences. Some had even unwittingly been schooling themselves for leadership roles and preparing themselves for the necessary costs and sacrifices they would be required to make to achieve a position of leadership. How then can we offer to teach more appropriate behaviors?

We discovered that it is not necessary to have gone through all those experiences to acquire behaviors relevant to coping with ambiguity and to feeling more relaxed about the uncertainty it produces. We've borrowed from the extensive research in leadership, and we've added our own views bolstered by talking to people in roles with considerable ambiguity and uncertainty. We've also constructed questionnaires and surveys, completed structured interviews, and applied vast numbers of mind-numbing statistical techniques to the data to be sure that the behavioral analysis we offer in Chapters 3 and 4 are not only psychologically sound, but statistically significant.

Where are the role models?

Wouldn't it be nice if life were like a "feel-good" movie? You know that in the early parts of the film our hero or heroine will go through all kinds of trials and difficulties, but by the end of the last reel things will work out fine. Oh, if only ... In a book on uncertainty we certainly can't promise you a happy ending every time! But what we *can* offer is a helping hand. By following our analysis of uncertain situations and the behavior that works with them, we believe that you can handle uncertainty more effectively.

> Ambiguity is a place where opportunity lives.

This book offers three ways that you can be more relaxed in handling the uncertainty you feel when facing life's ambiguities. First, we've identified the key skills and capabilities – and most of the important behaviors that go with them – that help people relax when handling their uncertainty. We'll then describe some very practical ways that you can enhance your ability with those particular behaviors and thus develop your competence in those areas. Finally, we'll show you how to assess the leadership context in which you find yourself and how to choose and use appropriate behaviors to match that context.

Why relax?

With more choice and greater ambiguity in our lives, the rules that used to help us understand and operate in our world no longer seem to apply. We need behaviors that work in a rule-changing – maybe even a rule-free – world. Not only this, but have you noticed how the best athletes, the best artists, arguably the best performers at anything, work well in a relaxed state? The world calls for higher and higher performance in whatever field you operate. How will you achieve that in your life without being relaxed? Relaxation is preparation for high performance. But it is not a relaxation of ignoring the issues or abandoning the problems and not making the best use of all available information. Instead, it's a relaxation that recognizes that ambiguity is a place where opportunity lives. The people who can move toward the ambiguity conquer their feelings of uncertainty and are relaxed enough to achieve the highest performance.

Notes

1.   Peters, T.J. and Waterman, R.H. (1982) *In Search of Excellence*. New York: Harper & Row.

2. McCall, M.W. Jr., Lombardo, M.M. and Morrison, A.M. (1988) *The Lessons of Experience: How Successful Executives Develop on the Job.* Lexington, MA: Lexington Books.

3. Margerison, C.J. (1980) "Leadership paths and profiles," in *Leadership and Organization Development*, Vol. 1, No. 1, pp. 12–17.

CHAPTER 1

HOW OLD IS NEW?

When we finished writing this book, Randy was 48 years old and Phil was 52. By the standards of many organizations and people we've described in the book, we're old!

In an earlier draft we wrote about all the "new" aspects of work and organizational life that we had seen in our working lives. As we related these changes to one of our colleagues Pradeep – 31 years old at the time – his reaction was, "It's not new, that's all I've ever known, it's ordinary." Although we care dearly about all of our readers, we don't actually think it matters whether you find today's organizational and business circumstances staggeringly new or tediously normal. What does matter is taking on the right behavior to deal with the issues and problems that you face as a manager and leader in your organization.

It's what you do, not what you meant to do

People judge you on your behavior, not your intentions. We've identified the behaviors, skills, and attitudes needed whenever rapid change produces high levels of ambiguity. So potentially, this book could have been useful at any point in history when these conditions were true. We certainly believe that the behaviors, skills, and attitudes would continue to be relevant into the future. So whoever you are and whatever experiences you have had, if you find yourself facing ambiguity and not feeling relaxed about coping with your own uncertainty, we think the material in this book will be relevant to you.

It is true that many of the people we talked to (many of them are closer to our age rather than Pradeep's) are reeling from the shock of what they see as continually increasing change. Our observations are that the skills and behaviors we describe for dealing with ambiguity are not widely practiced, or done well, or always valued. We trust that this

> The skills and behaviors for dealing with ambiguity are not widely practiced, or done well, or always valued.

situation will change because we firmly believe that without applying the kinds of skills we describe, all kinds of organizations will suffer and not be able to cope in the current – let alone the future – world.

Who are we writing for?

We think the people who will be most attracted to the ideas in this book fall into four categories:

1. **High-flyers** Ambitious people who need to be on top of the latest thinking in management and leadership and are keen to apply it. They probably have an MBA or have educated themselves to an equivalent level. They reference global resources relating to business and world affairs. They expect rigorous research. They will have had at least one significant managerial step so far in their careers and most likely are already looking for their next major career move. These are the people who are going to go on to become the chief executives, senior vice-presidents and senior civil servants. They recognize that their life is about handling pressure, not just within work, but also finding some form of harmony between the pressures of their existing and future roles and those they also occupy outside of work, with family and in the community.

2. **High-learners** People who have even greater curiosity than ambition, but in most other respects are similar to the high-flyers. They're fascinated by their current field of work; they may be in a professional partnership, such as accounting, engineering, or law – or they may be internal consultants. They may be employed in an organization to develop their specialist expert knowledge, and they may just be bumping into the realization that expertise doesn't get you everywhere in senior management. They have already experienced the need to significantly modify their skill set to take on higher levels of responsibility.

3. **High-worriers** These people are concerned about the rate of change in their organization and probably in their industry. They may have worked in that industry or field for a long time and be worried about their ability to keep up with the pace of organizational and individual change. They are looking for solutions, and while they would prefer something quick and simple to implement, they are probably mature enough by now to realize that the solutions to their problems need more effort and will turn out to be more complex than they first hoped. They find the imposition of change through industry mergers, major shifts in the market, government changes of legislation, and so on, to be disturbing because they appear to have no influence or power at all over the changes that occur. What they can do is have a lot of influence about how they handle the change and its impact on themselves and their colleagues.

4. **High-carers** Often found in human resources departments, these are the people developers and people sponsors in organizations and communities. They're always looking for people who can grow and develop. They genuinely believe that people are an organization's biggest asset. They look for opportunities to offer the latest and most usable thinking to their people and their colleagues and delight in helping them grow and develop. They are not always very good at developing themselves and sometimes find themselves unprepared for changes that they personally need to make.

Finding answers to the questions

When people hear that we research, teach, and consult in the area of leadership, there are a number of questions they almost always raise. In addition, when they hear that we research ambiguity and uncertainty, that throws a few more questions into the conversation. We'd like to raise these issues and help you think about your own answers to these questions.

What's the difference between leadership and management?

When anybody talks about leadership, the questions of what is leadership and what is management inevitably arise. We will deal with these questions at greater length in Chapter 5, but just in case you can't wait until then, here are a couple of pointers. If you're collecting butterflies and you're into taxonomy, then classification is important. However, most of the people we meet nowadays are more concerned with what they need to do or to learn to get the job done. Our approach, therefore, is to look for useful behaviors, not worry about what we call them. As a dot.com startup manager we spoke to said, "I have a hundred decisions to make before lunch time. I don't care if I'm called a leader or a cleaner, as long as I make good decisions." We take the same view.

If you really *must* define things like this, then take a leaf out of the biologist's book. The word *leadership* is roughly equivalent to the biological term *mammals*, and *management* is roughly equivalent to the biological term *animals*. So in biological terms, it's fair to say that mammals are animals. But how much has that helped you? You have to get much more precise and much more detailed before you are describing anything useful.

> "I have a hundred decision to make before lunch time. I don't care if I'm called a leader or a cleaner, as long as I make good decisions."

Is this about the real world?

If the question means: have we invented all this in a parallel universe inhabited solely by theoretical models? Then the answer is no, we haven't. It all comes from real conversations with real people in real organizations. If the question means: is everyone already using these behaviors? The answer is, no, definitely not. Our evidence and the work of Moses and colleagues at AT&T[1] suggest that no more than 10 to 15 percent of the highest potential middle to senior managers apply the skills of handling uncertainty and ambiguity. So the behaviors that we're describing and the routes to improving the skill level of those behaviors will be something that is new to many managers.

But you say none of these behaviors are new. Aren't they being used already?

Taxes, smart phones, and gravity only became obvious once they were pointed out. Because something is known, it appears not to be new. However, our research in over 30 countries and in more than 100 organizations suggests that while these ideas may be known, they are not widely practiced.

I know what I want to do, but how do I do it?

This is exactly our point. For years, if not decades, managers have been besieged by good and useful advice telling them what to do. You've had *what* to dos – in strategy, marketing, human resources, systems, operations, finance, absolutely everything – but very little on *how* to do it. How do you approach the implementation of strategy? How do you empower people in such a way that they actually do what needs to be done? By tackling the apparently mundane level of behavior, we are attempting to provide our readers with a genuine set of workable skills that they can apply immediately, and which will enhance the rest of their lives and careers.

The advice to managers and leaders has been about what to do, not *how* to do it. We have seen reengineering, transformation, re-invention, new, speed, competencies, teachable points of view, destroying your business, BHAGs (big hairy audacious goals)[2] – they're all about what is *supposed* to happen. But very little has been said about exactly how you do it. What are the minute and detailed behaviors necessary to accomplish these wonderful things? That's what this book is about.

Is it just behavior?

We'd love to invent a new word for this section. The behavior we describe will only be effective if it is done to a certain skill level. Ensuring that behavior is practiced until it becomes skillful needs some repetition and perhaps even a tolerance for risking new behavior. The support for these repetitions and practice will come from having the right attitude. The attitude will support you. So really, we'd like to invent a new word, something that combines attitude and skill, i.e. "skattitude." Alas, we think it's unlikely to catch on, so we'll stick with our mixture of behaviors, skills and attitudes.

What is the link between uncertainty, ambiguity and chaos?

There are mathematical theories of chaos and complexity. They require high levels of mathematical skill and knowledge, and in our view – lovely though the metaphors are that spring from them, and we hope that butterflies are still doing well in Brazil – we haven't found much that is directly transferable from the chaos and complexity worlds to the behavioral world we have been studying. However, this doesn't prevent us from wanting to borrow the metaphors from time to time.

Coping or deliberate?

Sometimes ambiguity is unavoidable – forced on you, if you like – and therefore your behavior is about coping with the uncertainty that you feel. However, there will be other occasions when you choose to move towards the ambiguity as a deliberate strategy. This is where moving towards ambiguity starts to emerge as a leadership style in its own right. This kind of leadership style makes huge demands on learning ability, but it can also be very exciting. We call it the "learning leadership style," and we describe it in much more detail in Chapter 5.

Does this cover all leadership styles?

No, it doesn't. Indeed some of the widely discussed and understood requirements of leaders – courage, ability to handle strategy, developing trust, etc. – are hardly discussed at all because they are well covered elsewhere. We are interested in two different dimensions. The first is how people handle uncertainty, whatever their leadership and management styles. We have identified eight sets of specific, learnable behaviors that make handling uncertainty more effective – we call them "Enablers." We have also identified eight behaviors that prevent you from handling uncertainty in a relaxed style – we call them "Restrainers." Enablers and Restrainers, are dealt with in detail in Chapters 3 and 4, together with a wide range of practical suggestions for how you can improve your skill in using these behaviors. In Chapter 5 we discuss how the use of Enablers constitutes a new leadership style, and how that style fits in with leadership styles that have been identified by other leadership researchers and writers.

> Moving towards ambiguity starts to emerge as a leadership style in its own right.

Send in the metaphors

But surely if this is a book about leading, according to what I read in most leadership books, I'm supposed to charge with the buffaloes, swim with the dolphins, create a burning platform, hunt with the tigers, bite with the sharks. All as written up by a Chinese warrior-philosopher, in no more than a minute, rounded off by seven homely stories of effective chief executives who made good on Mars and Venus.

OK. If you want metaphors, you can have metaphors.

Think about an increasing level of global ambiguity (like global warming) that has produced a rise in the sea levels of uncertainty. The inhabitants of the planet, having previously been accustomed to life on firm ground, now need to adapt to the more fluid environment in which they find themselves. Unfortunately, all their habits, behaviors, instincts and attitudes have been based on living on solid ground. Now they are going to adapt to a world where many of the rules are different from the ones they grew up with. How do we help those people to become as relaxed with the new environment as they were with the old?

At this point feel free to throw in, go with the flow, swim with the tide, and avoid being set adrift. Problems now represent the risk of over immersion, drowning and being swamped. Routes to survival and success will involve learning better swimming techniques, being at home in the water, inventing aqualungs and breathing techniques, and continually developing skills. We are sure you are well ahead of us in envisaging a new world where the aquatic and flexible citizens live happy and fulfilled lives because they have adapted to their new environment, not by giving up any of their old skills, but by adding to them and modifying the instincts that went with them and the attitudes that controlled those instincts.

There – now don't you feel much better?

Two kinds of ambiguity and uncertainty

We mentioned in the Introduction that ambiguity is how it is and uncertainty is how you feel about it. We now want to point out that there are actually two kinds of ambiguity in the world. What we are calling Ambiguity Type 1 and Ambiguity Type 2.

- **Ambiguity Type 1** Imagine you are lost in a big city. Perhaps it is raining and you can't get a taxi, but you've still got to find your way to a particular location. What do you do? Hopefully you can ask directions from passers-by, check an app, use bus and train information to help you, ask in a shop or some official who might know. The situation is one where you are uncertain, but there are other people or other ways of finding out the data you need. The way to eliminate your uncertainty is to find an expert. The expertise may be with the individual, a system or written down in some form. So the solution to this kind of problem is to find a source of expertise that meets your needs.

- **Ambiguity Type 2** What will your customers need 20 years from now? While you don't know, you are also aware that no one else knows either. It's also true that there may be several "right" answers to this question. So although many people may have strong views and trust their intuition and make imaginative suggestions, no one actually knows. The consequence of this kind of uncertainty is that your views and approach may be as relevant as anybody else's. You are, like Indiana Jones, "making it up as you go." Paradoxically, by being out front with your conjecture, you may be defining the marketplace for all competitors now and 20 years hence!

However, you are vulnerable. You will have experienced many examples of uncertainty where the correct solution is to find the expert. Many kinds of uncertainty may at first seem as if they should be Type 1, and therefore your solution is to search for the expert. In practice they turn out to be Type 2, where searching for experts will do you very little good. In fact, it may even do you harm because you may suffer from what we call the "false guru syndrome."

False gurus are people who have strong views, may have been experts in the past, and may have known useful things in the past, but are now in a field where no one can reasonably know what needs to be known. All they can do is to make suggestions and voice opinions, even though those opinions may have no greater validity than your own. Yet, being accompanied by all the trappings of the guru, and amplified by your understandable need to find an expert, it's very easy to take advice, even pay for advice, which is no better than you could have given yourself.

In this book we are mainly going to look at Ambiguity Type 2. It's the kind of uncertainty that individuals and organizations face where everything is new and where no one has exactly faced these circumstances before. While we don't want to decry the use of expertise when the expertise is valid, we do want to caution you on depending on expertise that may no longer be relevant. What we want to do is arm you with skills that make for survival and growth in a grown-up, messy world.

However, there is an historical note here. If today no one knows something, by tomorrow someone might. And therefore the problem moves from a Type 2 to a Type 1 Ambiguity. It may then be possible to solve the uncertainty using some technique, method, or knowledge that has recently been discovered. Few things remain unknown forever. The danger is that the expert will assume that because something worked in one situation, that solution will transfer to the next situation (see Chapter 4). Chaos theory points out to us that in chaotic situations and on the edge of chaotic situations the starting situation is never the same between two circumstances, so the outcome need never be predicted and the solution to achieve the desired outcome will need to be created on each new occasion.

What questions do people ask when facing ambiguity and uncertainty?

You should be able to answer these questions for yourself.

When we explain to people that we research ambiguity and uncertainty, people ask us a lot of "how to" questions. These are the most common:

- *How can I be more relaxed and confident about the ambiguities that I face at work, so that I will be an even better manager and leader?*

- *Uncertainty really screws me up. How can I feel more comfortable with it?*

- *I feel unable to cope with the (new) business environment. What can I do?*

- *How do I lead my part of the organization better?*

- *How do I create a workplace that is energized and motivated, given the dramatic changes that we've all been through and will continue to go through?*

- *How do I take my organization into the unknown?*

- *How do I get into an unfamiliar (to me) business and get on top of it quickly?*

22

- *How can I achieve what I am aiming for?*
- *What can I do to achieve my long-term goals?*
- *How do I admit what I don't know?*

The real work of leadership

When we originally tackled this topic in 1996, our definition of this emerging leadership style was:

> *The leader's role is to identify productive areas of uncertainty and confusion and to lead the organization into those areas to gain competitive (or other kinds of) advantage.*[3]

If opportunity is to be found in ambiguity by overcoming the natural sense of uncertainty, then leaders of the future will head towards ambiguity more and more frequently. In the end, leadership is not a status, it's a state of mind, and the relaxed leader is likely to be the most effective. In the next chapter we will show you how to become more relaxed while you learn. After all, uncertainty is the opportunity to learn.

Notes

1. Moses, J and Lyness, K. (1990) "Leadership behavior in ambiguous environments," in Clark, K.E. and Clark M.E. (eds), *Measures of Leadership*. West Orange, N.J.: Leadership Library of America, pp. 327–37.

2. Collins, J. C. and Porras, J. I. (1994) *Built to Last: Successful Habits of Visionary Companies*. New York: HarperCollins Publishers.

3. White, R. P., Hodgson, E and Crainer, S. (1996) *The Future of Leadership: Riding the Corporate Rapids into the 21st Century*. London: Pitman Publishing.

CHAPTER 2

THE REAL CHANGE SALOON

To make best use of the behaviors and skills that we describe in this book, we would like you to think about the assumptions about effective leadership you carry with you. As Bill Sternbergh, our former colleague at the Center for Creative Leadership, frequently says, "If you do what you've always done, you'll get what you always got." If you really want to check into the Real Change Saloon, you're going to need to leave your old assumptions at the doorway.

> If you do what you've always done, you'll get what you always got.

Without the use of drugs or metaphysical experiences, could you step outside your mind for a moment, please? Difficult, isn't it? Yet unless we all step outside our minds, how else do we check whether what we are doing is really appropriate to the moment or simply a repeat of behavior patterns we learned long ago? Often we find that we continue outdated and outmoded behavior because we have failed to check the assumptions about what is or is not appropriate. And yes, we will be asking you to step outside your mind, because we've found a marvelous way of doing it. It's called "thinking like a child."

Try to imagine that you are having a conversation with a small child, probably in the range of six to ten years old. Children of this age are usually very curious and usually very good at asking difficult questions. We find childlike questions are some of the most powerful that are available, so the child is going to ask you some questions. In our experience, the most effective consultants or managers – in fact, anyone who asks questions as part of their work – are people who ask childlike questions from time to time because they often get to the deeper issues underlying a problem. We have selected six childlike questions to identify the areas where we believe people may be in danger of carrying forward assumptions (some would say illusions) from the previous century, which will not work in the present one. So before reading anything else, take a moment to check out those assumptions.

Damaging illusions from the twentieth century

Why do you believe you are in control?

The more senior you are, the more powerful you are. The more powerful you are, the more control you have. Or so the theory goes. Think of the people you work with. How many of them behave as if they control things, when in practice what they actually do is issue instructions and complaints? Even if they had the power to insist and tell people what to do, would things work out the way they mandated? One of the ironies of achieving top management levels in most organizations is that although the trappings of power and influence are there, in practice the use of that power, except in relatively rare situations, is unlikely to work in a positive way. You can order people about for only so long, then they leave.

Why do you behave as if you can predict the future, its consequences and outcomes?

Do you prepare budgets? That's a prediction of the future. Do you draw up business plans? How far ahead? Now who is fooling whom here? To what extent can you forecast the future? Can you forecast what your competitors will do or what new start-up will threaten you? To what extent can you be certain – really certain – of the future? We hope your honest answer to this question is that it's less and less possible to predict the future – you can't see the end from the beginning. Of course, there is nothing wrong with planning – planning helps you prepare. The illusion we are concerned about is that, by drawing up detailed plans, organizations and their managers behave as if they can predict the future and in this way can tell when things are not going according to plan. Compounding the issue, they assume the plan is the only way that the future can unravel. Our point is that when heading towards greater levels of uncertainty, you will only be relaxed if you can cope with the possibility of many different futures – each with its own positives and negatives unfolding as more information and data becomes available. Sure you can make some "guesstimates," and of course, you can make some scenario-based conclusions. But if you go back over the last three years of your organization's history,

> When heading towards greater levels of uncertainty, you will only be relaxed if you can cope with the possibility of many different futures.

how many times have people been able to predict exactly what was going to happen, as opposed to some very approximate trends? Additionally, how many times have you had to modify your activities or your plans in light of things cropping up that were unforeseen?

Why do you think that because you've done it before and it worked that it will work again?

There's something about experts here. Experts are people who have learned that there is a better answer, even a best answer, to a particular problem or issue. As ambiguity increases, the chances of the situation repeating itself reduce. Theorists of mathematical chaos say that if you can't describe accurately the starting position of a system, you can't forecast the precise outcome of that system. We notice so many people who carry the assumption that there is one best answer to a problem – the magic bullet – and it is there to be found somewhere. So they devote a large part of their efforts to searching for the solution. There is also a need to find experts and rely on them. Expertise increases certainty – or does it? Experts will continue to be useful as long as their expertise is still appropriate. But in many technical areas, expertise becomes out-of-date almost before it is understood by the majority. The geneticist, the software writer, the retail marketer, the advertising creative – all have to continually keep their technical expertise up-to-date. Taking even a short break from the detail of their work will mean that the detail is different when they return. Beware the doctor or dentist – or any professional – who does not challenge and review the techniques they learned at college.

Why do you believe everything important is measurable?

The influential Lord Kelvin, president in 1895 of Britain's most prestigious scientific body, The Royal Society, gave considerable credence to this belief. (He did, after all, come up with the Kelvin scale for measuring temperature.) He was quoted as saying, "To measure is to know," and "if you cannot measure it, you cannot improve it." He was talking about the physical sciences, and of course, it's useful to be able to measure things and for the measurements to be useful information. Sadly, with the manipulation of statistics having become so prevalent, we suspect that sometimes measurements devalue rather than add value. Yes, of course, you need to measure company results, human performance, market shares, stock price levels, and so on. And yes, of course, you can plot graphs of these things and make guesses about what will go up and what will go down. But if you genuinely believe that what gets measured gets done, how do people achieve trust in your organization? How do they achieve higher quality in their communication? How do they instill hope and enthusiasm when things get difficult? How do they re-motivate themselves following a slump? None of these is measurable except by some form of survey, which puts an imposed scale on a basic human emotion – motivation. Why don't we allow human emotion to be part of our management process?

> Expertise increases certainty – or does it?

Why do you think that words like leadership, management, and change have the same meaning for everyone?

You know from even the briefest conversations with colleagues and friends that everyone has a different definition of leadership. No one agrees what management is and isn't, and as for change, one person's high-stress, high-pressure change is another person's boring day. Yet why do we operate as if these words have absolute and unchanging meaning? Is it really the case that what was good leadership behavior at the turn of the twentieth century will be good leadership behavior at the turn of the twenty-first century?

Why do you think that reducing uncertainty will necessarily increase certainty?

Yes, of course, in some cases it does. If you can avoid the mistakes you made last time, you will decrease the uncertainty with which you put together that plan and implemented that strategy. But removing uncertainty may not increase the certainty. It may not help you know what you should do, merely what you should not do. In a world where the level and range of choice is overwhelming, eliminating what not to do still leaves you with a vast array of choices. Imagine you are buying a car. On the sales lot are 50 cars, each of which could fit your needs. Which do you choose? First, you eliminate ten because of size, ten because of cost, and five because you don't like the color, but that still leaves you with 25 cars to choose from. Knowing what you don't like or what is not appropriate does not necessarily narrow down your decision to one option. You still have to make an active choice. In our research on becoming more relaxed with uncertainty, we have discovered that attempts to make life more certain simply by concentrating on reducing uncertainty is only part of the solution.

The ABCs of enhancement

Have you ever wanted to be better at something? The next chapter introduces skills that will help you be more relaxed when facing ambiguity and uncertainty. They are not simple skills. They also rely on having the right attitude. In this chapter we want to prepare you to develop the appropriate skills and attitudes as practicable behaviors. In some cases just doing more of the behavior will be fine, but in other cases you need to examine your attitude so you can develop behavior to the necessary level of skill.

We have deliberately chosen to talk about enabling your behavior and skills. We believe that most of the skills and behaviors we are referring to are not in fact new – you probably use many of them already. Even if you don't, you probably used them at some point when you were younger. It is our belief that children are frequently more able to cope with ambiguity and uncertainty than adults. If you think about a child who is five or six years old, most of life for that child is filled with uncertainty and ambiguity. One of the ways you can view the role of parenting is that of helping your child move from a state of almost continual uncertainty to one of some level of certainty.

We have found it useful to make the assumption that all of our clients have been children once. This may be an extravagant assumption in one or two cases, but the serious point is that as a child you probably had ambiguity coping skills in at least as good a state as you have them now – probably better in many cases. We don't expect to teach people many new skills, but we do expect to help them recover and enhance the skills they once had.

28

It seems a sad reflection on our lives that for the most part growing up involves avoiding more uncertainty rather than less. Our point is that the process of improving your ability to handle these skills may not be one of learning a new skill. In most cases we believe it is much more likely that you are going to be unearthing a skill that you once had but have to some degree buried. This will often require a different development process than the process you used at school, where the aim was to teach you new skills. The issue, then, is to unearth these skills, rediscover them and enhance them – perhaps even rethinking them to fit into the new context in which you operate. Our assumption is that the uncertainty skills you might have been using at the age of six would have been operating in a different context from the ones you use today. Please assure us that the playground uncertainties you suffered as a six-year-old are not remotely similar to the ones you are facing in the boardroom 30 or more years later!

But first, we need to digress ... How do you enhance your skills? Could it really be as easy as A, B, C?

Attitude matters

It has long been known that if you want to do something – let us say, learn to play the guitar – then the attitude you have towards learning the skills and behaviors associated with playing the guitar will influence your willingness to practice and in general terms will increase or decrease your preparedness to put in the work and behavior needed to become skillful. For example, as a child, a teacher or parent may have insisted that you learn to play an instrument. You disliked the instrument from the moment you picked it up, and you were forced to practice every day after school. You did everything you could to minimize the practice time. Lo and behold, you stopped playing the instrument as soon as you possibly could. On the other hand, a little later in life, you thought it might be good to take it up again. You were interested. You wanted to. You knew your friends would be impressed if you could strum a few chords. So you practiced. You put in at least a minimum of effort which allowed you to develop some skill with the instrument. Ah ... so attitude matters!

We are interested in attitude from the point of view that in learning and enhancing a skill, your attitude is crucial in two ways. First, our research suggests that it is not just the behavior that

Ah ... so attitude matters!

29

matters, but it is the attitude underlying the behavior that will influence how other people respond to you. So you are not just learning a skill, but you are learning to enjoy using that skill. The greater your enjoyment of the skill, the higher the likelihood others will respond positively. Second (and we will come to this shortly), your motivation to continue enhancing this skill in the face of difficulties will be directly proportional to the attitude of enthusiasm that you bring to that task.

Behavior counts

All of the skills in this book involve behaviors that are observable. In many cases we are going to describe the particular behaviors that you could learn immediately to help deal more effectively with ambiguity. For instance, one of the signs of a "Mystery-Seeker" is that even when they know how to do something, they will try a different way, just to test out themselves or their ideas (*see* Chapter 3). This is something you could try out immediately. When offered a comfortable solution, you could reject it and start searching for another solution. This behavior itself does not necessarily mean that you will produce a better solution, but at least you are looking for it, which is the key. Another example, "constantly listens for faint signals of what may become significant," is something you can also do immediately because you can start looking to the future right now. Start by writing down five things that you feel will influence your business or the way you do business over the next ten years. Set aside some time in your daily schedule for thinking about the future. Use the phrase "what if." All these things will contribute immediately to your effectiveness in scanning ahead, a critical skill in dealing with ambiguity. A key point is that you don't have to go through years of attitude change to start working on a new behavior. However, there is a third component in dealing with behavioral change.

Capability: how good can it get?

The capability to do something is behavior plus skill and experience. "Shifts gears to handle several levels of risk" is not something you can do without some skill or practice (*see* Chapter 3). It takes know-how and experience to be able to shift gears easily. It is not a simple behavior that can just be applied from day one. "Good at constructing scenarios about the way things might be" involves an ability to create a scenario that other people will appreciate (*see* Chapter 3). Just to make the point, if we had said, "Constructs scenarios about the way things might be," then that would simply be a behavior. It may not involve producing *good* scenarios at all. To become *good* at constructing future scenarios, you need to practice until you become skilled.

The route to enhancing skills is going to be somewhat different for each of the eight Enablers. In some cases, where there are straightforward behaviors that can be adopted and used immediately, then enhancement will be rapid. In other cases, where a capability is being described, then the route to that capability (like guitar playing, soccer playing, juggling) is practice, practice, practice! You start with a simple behavior and practice it until you get better. In most cases, there will be some kind of attitude that influences the way the behavior is done and the way the capability is developed. It may take some time before you are able to say, "The harder things get, the more energy I have," but we are confident that with lots of practice and the right motivation, improvement will be possible.

> Attitude + Behavior + Practice (or experience) = Capability

The MBE of action

You've enhanced your skills, but will you start to use them and continue to use them? Only if you are *motivated* to start, have removed the *blockages* to action, and have *encouragement* to continue.

Motivation

Humans are supreme learning animals. They continue to learn, even in the poorest of conditions. However, if you need to learn something new, particularly if that something is a little difficult, the process is much easier if you are keen and motivated.

If you're trying to develop and train any kind of animal – and let's take one of the most intelligent, the dolphin – then punishment doesn't work. The only thing that works is reward. We understand from dolphin trainers that there is only one way you get a dolphin to jump and do all the fabulous tricks they do. Every time the animal moves towards the point you want it to, you reward it with a treat, i.e. fish. And you associate that reward with a particular action – possibly a signal like a whistle. In that way, you gradually encourage the animal to make the jump or do whatever is needed. This has been known for years among animal trainers. Sadly, it seems to be easily forgotten when humans are the learners. It is so easy for people to believe that reward and punishment stimulate the best learning. Don't believe it – only rewarding will work. But who wants to be a dolphin? Well, try treating yourself to some days as a dolphin and only get rewards, and then check your level of motivation.

Blockages to action

In Chapters 3 and 4, we offer a wide range of ideas labeled "Explore and Expand." These are suggestions for learning and practicing the behaviors we describe. If you are tempted to glance through but do nothing about them, take a moment now to ask yourself what might cause you to stop before trying out one or two of the suggestions. Let us make a guess. You're afraid of failing; you feel that you've not done anything quite like this before; that you'll look an idiot; that things will go wrong; that you'll get blamed. In short, the world will be a worse place as a result of you testing out some of these ideas. Of course, we sympathize. But do not flee in the face of these age-old objections to anything new. If you choose the right situation, where there is no major risk, then if something goes wrong, you won't actually look an idiot to anyone but yourself. And hopefully, you could live with that.

You can make it a lot safer by starting with suggestions that are easy and by doing them in small steps. If you've never done the behavior before, recognize that most of the future hasn't been done before either and you're going to get there somehow! Also take consolation from the fact that our evidence strongly suggests that you have done some of these behaviors before, but when you were much, much younger.

Encouragement

We see motivation as the push that *gets* you going and encouragement as the pull that *keeps* you going. So if you're taking on something new, how do you plan to have and enjoy your successes? Ian McDermott, CEO of ITS training and one of Europe's foremost NLP gurus, says that there's everything to play for, not work at. If there's something important to be done, the better way is to play at it rather than to work at it. Yes, we know that statement goes against a vast history of the work ethic, but think about it – when are you at your best? Is it when you are straining, tired, pressured and stressed, or could it be when you are feeling light, nimble, witty, amusing, playful, energetic – in short *relaxed?* So what to do? Approach other people who are good at this skill and ask them if they could show you how they do it – maybe even how they learned to do it.

Our experience has been that people love being asked how they do things when the mere question implies that they do it well.

> If there's something important to be done, the better way is to play at it rather than work at it.

As far as encouragement is concerned, arrange lots and lots of opportunities for feedback. Ask people how you're getting on. Set up some formats for yourself (there will be more detail on this in Chapter 3) that give you feedback on progress and that give you ways of analyzing your development and what has worked and what hasn't. The more you can trust the feedback, the more you can be encouraged by it, as every improvement will make a difference.

Some hard truths about developing yourself Remember ...

1. If you want to do something, you'll find it much easier if your attitude encourages you.

2. You can make a slight enhancement immediately to all of these skills simply by copying effective behaviors of other people.

3. You can develop the skill without changing the attitude – but it won't be so easy or appear genuine to other people.

4. Modifying the attitude may feel more risky, but needn't take any longer than learning the skill.

5. Just try it. Use some of the safeguards we suggest and work in comfortable learning steps appropriate to your current skill level. You might even enjoy it!

We opened this chapter by presenting six damaging illusions of the twentieth century because we believe that in a world of unprecedented choice and consequent opportunities for change, the assumptions that worked very well for us in previous decades will work less and less well for us now and in the future. These illusions block our ability to change by sapping our energy for change with beliefs that will prove to be falsehoods. We are not suggesting that you abandon all of them immediately – even if you could. We are all creatures of habit and these won't be easy to give up. However, we would like to signal them early on as potential areas of difficulty for all of us in learning to deal with uncertainty.

Additionally, we have detailed a strategy for enhancing/improving Enabler skills. We see these as critical to thriving in the coming decades, whether leader, follower, or individual contributor. In fact, we see these as survival skills for life.

CHAPTER 3

WHAT ARE ENABLERS?

Enablers are the skills and capabilities that will enable you to embrace ambiguity and handle your own uncertainty. Let's get to know them and find out what Enablers can do for you.

What does each Enabler do?

An Enabler is a group of attitudes and behaviors that helps you address ambiguity and stay relaxed about your own uncertainty. Chapter 3 is devoted to helping you to understand each Enabler and will give illustrations of what each Enabler looks like in action. You can get an approximate picture of yourself and your likelihood of having the Enabler skills and behaviors by going through the checklists throughout Chapter 3. (A much more detailed tool – The Ambiguity Architect™ – exists which will give a more complete picture.[1]) We have tried to be very practical throughout this book, and therefore we spend relatively little time debating whether your personality is or is not likely to make you better or worse at handling uncertainty. What we know is that certain behaviors help people face ambiguity in a more relaxed way. Therefore, the issue is, can you comfortably adopt some of those behaviors and incorporate them into your normal way of working, thinking, acting, and leading?

There is a real-life case study to illustrate each Enabler. These stories are based on real clients and research subjects we have worked with. We have changed names and some of the biographic and background details to ensure that the confidentiality agreements we have with our clients are not broken. So although the names are false, be assured the people and situations are real.

At the end of each Enabler profile we give you ideas labeled "Explore and expand" to help you develop and enhance your skills in these Enabler behaviors.

Are some Enablers more important than others?

We do not distinguish a hierarchy in these eight Enablers – at least, not clearly. You can read about them in whichever order appeals to you. Typically, we find most managers are skillful in two or three of the Enablers and equally have blind spots in two or three others. Flip through the pages and look at the ones that intrigue you most, possibly even horrify you most. Follow your instincts towards the things that you seem to know least about. That's the best way to stay relaxed with uncertainty.

ENABLER 1

MOTIVATED BY MYSTERIES

*Once you eliminate the impossible, whatever remains, no matter
how improbable, must be the truth.*

Sherlock Holmes

Motivated by what?

Imagine that everything was attractive. Imagine that the more you didn't
know, the more you wanted to know. Imagine that maybe wanting to
know was too weak a description, there was a hunger to know that drove
you from whatever else you were doing and pushed you to continually
make further inquiries about the things that you didn't know. Imagine
insatiable curiosity. You are a **Mystery-Seeker**.

Mystery-Seekers are curious people who are attracted to areas and
problems that are unknown to them. They question a lot; they want to
know who, why, and how. They are always seeking to understand and at
the same time using that understanding to explore further. Frequently,
this exploration is of a playful nature. They experiment, they test things
out – they put themselves in the role of both the experimenter and experi-
mental subject. When they see a new building, they will stop and investigate it. They will take a new way home, just to see if it is more interesting.
They will explore a new road, just to see where it goes. When you go
for a walk with this person, they will continually be looking over fences,
wondering what is over the next hill or around the next bend. They will
want to change the walk based on what they've discovered and then to
modify it further to go and investigate something. They won't stick to

the plan if the plan prevents them from learning something or inquiring about something.

Mystery-Seekers encourage others to be challenged by the unknown. This can make for discomforting company. You thought you were going to a business meeting to confirm the budget for a particular project, but instead you end up being drawn into a debate about how that product could be modified and used to create a new market somewhere. In times of pressure this can be seen as disconcertingly unfocused. Yet people who are highly motivated by mysteries can be extremely focused. They are almost obsessive in wanting to know more and exploring the thing they don't yet know about. These people will also question things 'for the hell of it' and have been known to tear things up and start all over because they think it's the right thing to do.

Mystery-Seekers actually seem to get energy from not knowing. Most people get some satisfaction when they discover the solution to a problem, but people who are motivated by mysteries seem to draw their energy when they *don't* have a solution. Yes, of course, they get satisfaction like everyone else when they have solved a particular problem, but the solving doesn't stop there. Once they have a solution, they will look for a second solution: a better one. Once they have a second solution they will probably go on and look for a third and then a fourth. For people who are strongly motivated by mysteries, it is the absence of the solution – the absence of knowing how something works – that is the really attractive part.

People who have been motivated by mysteries over the centuries have shown this insatiable curiosity and drive to continue to want to understand, and then having understood, they will want to go deeper still. More than 400 years ago Galileo Galilei risked torture and imprisonment because the best solution he could find to explaining his astronomical observations was that the earth moved around the sun rather than, as the Bible implied, the other way around. His enormous curiosity kept him asking questions about sunspots, phases of the moon, the phases of Venus, the moons of Jupiter – he never stopped. Even when seriously ill and highly troubled by the pressure of the cardinal's inquisition, he continued to work on a theory about the trajectory of bodies fired from cannons.

Half a millennium later, British inventor and entrepreneur James Dyson, in struggling to make a vacuum cleaner that did not require a paper or cloth bag, made more than 5000 prototypes before he finally achieved the level of perfection he sought. Having made his first production model, he carried on developing new ideas, and improving what was already improved upon. Just two years after its launch, Dyson's first product (an upright model) became Britain's best-selling vacuum cleaner, overtaking sales of Electrolux, Hoover, and Panasonic. A cylinder model launched two years later achieved similar success. Passionate about design and engineering innovation, Dyson says that success is made of 99 percent failure. His persistent curiosity took his business to European brand leader in just five years against multinational competition.[2] He has since gone on to disrupt other established industries – and who knows what he might do next.

But these people are not necessarily inventors in the normal sense. What is fundamental about them is that they are drawn instinctively to the edge of their knowledge rather than the center of it. It is for this reason that we believe that being motivated by mysteries may well be one of the *fundamental* skills underlying the ability to handle uncertainty. Think back to when you were at school. Predominantly what you were taught were facts – things that the teacher (and the society that supported the teacher) was reasonably sure and secure about. During Galileo's time, the teacher was the Church, and the Church knew from its interpretation of the Bible certain astronomical "facts." Since everyone was taught these facts, they were accepted as "truth." Mystery-Seekers leave this comfortable and safe center ground of accepted "truth" and move to the edge of their knowledge and their learning. They ask "why?" and "what would happen if?" and in general, ask the difficult questions. Later we will return to this theme, as it seems to be a precursor to what we call "difficult learning."

> [Mystery Seekers] are drawn instinctively to the edge of their knowledge rather than the center of it.

Mystery-Seekers are ...

Mystery-Seekers are curious people who are attracted to areas that are unknown and to problems that appear to have no obvious solution.

Signs of Mystery-Seekers

Tell-tale signs

- Often playful – that is, playing with ideas, playing with possibilities, asking "What if?"

- Play devil's advocate very effectively.

- Appear to get energy from *not* knowing, rather than from knowing. The search for knowledge and the acquisition of knowledge appear to be the energizing forces.

- Appear strangely happy when things don't work out the first time because they reveal a deeper paradox within the available data or add to their understanding of what the phenomenon isn't, or why things won't work.

- Will try a different way, even if they know how to do something, just to test out themselves or their ideas.

Tell-tale actions

- Gravitate towards projects with an element of the unknown.

- Demonstrate curiosity about a wide range of things.

- Always seek to understand things and then to further that understanding.

- Experiment and even willingly include self as part of the experiment.

- Always explore, both in conversation and practical situations.

- Challenge others to do the same. (This can be quite disconcerting for people who like a routine and a fixed reliance on what they know.)

- Ask questions "for the hell of it."

- Obsessively pursue an idea, a question, or a paradox for longer and in greater depth than others would regard as reasonable.

Tell-tale phrases

- "Where does this lead?"

- "That's unusual, let's investigate it."

- "There's lots of dead ends on the road to discovering something useful."

- "I don't know why that happens, but it fascinates me."

Case study

The case of the arthritic cough

We didn't need to go at all. Most of us had exceeded our sales targets for the year and were still within our cost budgets. It had been a good year for all of us. We were looking forward to a good bonus and maybe a couple of games of sales-oriented golf. But Ken was insistent. Why did the customer 50 miles from Madrid buy three times as much of our least popular cough suppressant as any other pharmacy of that size in the whole of Europe?

I should say at this point, that we all know about Ken and his wild goose chases. Who could forget the fuss about an apparent doubling of some sales orders in the UK at a sales conference some years ago? It turned out that some of the UK purchasers were ordering in pounds weight, while of course their other European colleagues were ordering in kilos. A fair amount of embarrassment all around on that one, and Ken got his reputation of fearlessly chasing things that didn't turn out to be very useful after all. But Ken was undaunted, and a couple of years later his knack for asking questions and exploring offbeat areas of no interest to the rest of us pulled a winner. Ken said that he liked "turning over stones," and it was true – sometimes he did find something useful underneath them.

It was Ken after all who had discovered that a material in our packaging was reacting with a new entity that we were just putting on to the market. Because of his insistent and urgent action, we avoided damaging our reputation and losing hundreds of thousands of dollars on the launch.

Anyway, because we all liked Ken and he had helped many of us in the past – in fact, was still a mentor to several of us even now – we humored him. Privately, we felt that a small pharmacist outside Madrid was probably reselling or involved in some kind of scam and that it wasn't a big enough matter to get seriously worried about. But we had to have a regional managers meeting, and so we agreed to meet at a hotel not far from the pharmacy. There was some cost in this decision. For many of us it added about half a day to our journey, but we had had a good year, and basically we all went along for the ride.

Of course, we all had to visit the shop, and the pharmacist was completely overwhelmed when all these regional managers from one of his major suppliers turned up on his doorstep. We were fascinated how small his shop was – boxes were stacked everywhere at the back of the shop. This was a typical rural pharmacy, not only selling medicines and preventatives, but also playing a key part in village healthcare and social life. Customers came in not just to buy, but to explore, debate and argue about theirs and others' symptoms and the likely remedies. It was a kind of ongoing medical debate from the moment he opened his doors until the moment they closed.

It was actually quite easy to find out why sales of our cough product were high. Yes, the pharmacist said that several of his older customers – of which there were many – also found that our cough suppressant reduced the pain and swelling of their arthritis. So there was the explanation to the high sales.

"Problem solved," we all thought as we had lunch at our hotel. However, unlike everyone else, Ken was, if anything, even more curious than before. He kept pounding away at the problem. Why this village, this pharmacist, these old people? There were hundreds, no thousands, of similar pharmacies across Europe that had aging populations who suffered from arthritis. Why hadn't anyone else discovered this effect on arthritis? Were all the old people in the village we had just visited under some kind of illusion? Was there any genuine clinical benefit from our cough suppressant, or was it some kind of placebo effect? Ken looked happy that he (and we – after all, we came, didn't we?) had started exploring the problem and now this latest evidence showed that there was a deeper puzzle that he still could not solve.

The rest of us lost interest at this point. We came, we saw, we got an immediate answer that *seemed* to fit the facts. Time to move on to other things. We completed our busy agenda and moved on, forgetting the whole thing. It was three months later that I bumped into Ken; he grabbed me by the arm, clearly excited about something. We found a coffee machine and sat down nearby. Over a hot drink that bore some resemblance to coffee, he explained to me about the pharmacy and how he had continued to probe at the problem. This behavior didn't surprise me at all – I was just grateful that he hadn't involved the rest of us. But what Ken had discovered was something unique about the village we had visited. Although they were officially discouraged from using their old wells and springs now that the village had a public water supply, many of the older people ignored the official advice and still accessed water from the traditional sources in preference to the modern piped variety. Just that morning Ken had discovered that when the well and spring water was tested, it had a much higher than average potassium content. Now he had something to go on. Ken was putting together a paper to seek funding and a proper investigation on just what effect the potassium level and our cough suppressant were having.

Within the year, preliminary results showed a genuine positive impact. This gave the research team a major insight, which they have high hopes of turning into a drug that will have widespread application for the relief of arthritis. So much for a worthless trip into the hills outside Madrid. Ken had done it again!

What happens if no one is motivated by mysteries?

People who are not motivated by mysteries – who are not Seekers – use patterns of behavior in approaching the unknown that are narrow and unvarying. They aren't looking for variation in their life; in fact, they prefer things to be the same as they always were. They are not likely to go looking for new discoveries, new ideas, or some other variants in their lives. Sometimes this is a survival mechanism. If you have been living in a state of civil war for some several years, the last thing you want is more change. What you want is to go back to things as they were – to the stability and the certainty that you used to enjoy. However, with traumatic situations put aside, the danger for an individual, an organization or a society that is not motivated by mysteries is that they will be unaware of or unprepared to take up new ideas and changes that occur. Take a look at the graph from *The Economist*,[3] (*see* Fig. 3.1), which shows the hundreds of years of almost repetitive similarity followed by a brief century of such rapid change, that the graph almost goes off the page. People who lived in earlier centuries of the previous millennium could be forgiven for expecting that the world would be similar when they died to what it was when they were born. Clearly, that is not true now. Organizations that do not seek out the things they are unaware of become more vulnerable and as Darwin forecasted, will not survive if they are less fit than their new competitors.

An example of adjusting to change along these lines involves the *Encyclopaedia Britannica*. Around 270 years of publishing tomes convinced the *Encyclopaedia's* leadership that there would always be a need for solid, leather-bound volumes that would be updated by an annual volume containing the highlights of knowledge and events of the previous year. Because of this view of the world, they rejected the fledgling Microsoft Corporation's overture to produce a version on CD-ROM. *Encarta*, a competing product, was born as a result of this rejection, but of course, it didn't belong to *Britannica*. *Britannica* was then facing chaos as it tried to retrench and catch up with the revolution that had taken place in the

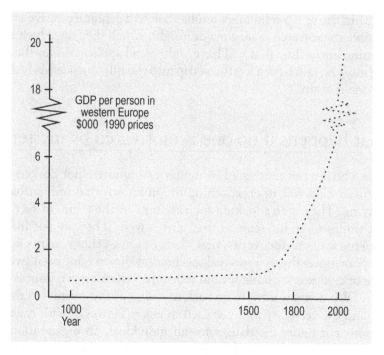

Figure 3.1 ♦ The growing rate of growth and change
Source: Adapted from *The Economists* 31 December 1999

knowledge marketplace. It is speculation, but if a member of the senior team had been more motivated by mysteries – had been attracted to taking a new way home, for instance – then wouldn't this crisis have been seen as an opportunity? Eventually, Britannica did find new opportunities by developing its own online Chrome extension that serves authoritative information alongside the standard search engine findings.

So it seems that being attracted by mysteries is one of the key aspects of living in and guiding any organization with prospects for long-term survival. However, what is it like if too many people nose around and inquire? Can't this get disruptive, too? Surely an organization needs to have a steady path. Although being motivated by mysteries is one of our fundamentals, we do not see it as the only essential skill. Clearly, if people spend their entire time being curious and pushing back boundaries, they may not have any

> "I have no special talents, I am only passionately curious ... the important thing is not to stop questioning." Albert Einstein.

time to focus on the things that matter in their own lives, in their own organizations, in their own societies. There has to be balance between curiosity and paying attention to important matters in the present.

Being motivated by mysteries is not a kind of "mad scientist syndrome;" it is a constant companion to everything else the individual surviving in uncertainty will do. But it should not be overplayed to such an extent that all other matters of everyday life, survival and planning ahead, are diminished. It is said that Albert Einstein, brilliant though he was, didn't know his own phone number or address. However, Einstein was clearly highly motivated by mysteries. He described himself and his approach in this way: "I have no special talents, I am only passionately curious" and "the important thing is not to stop questioning." In everyday usage, being motivated by mysteries is about being attracted by the unknown aspects of new sources of data, new ideas or new opportunities. But it is also about integrating that curiosity into the rest of the skills and operations that we need to use. It's about being fluid: the great ideas of tomorrow are the questions of today.

Difficult learning

An additional aspect of being motivated by mysteries is a concept we first introduced in our previous book *The Future of Leadership*. We named the concept "difficult learning." It has been our experience that those people and organizations that embrace uncertainty are often drawn to doing things, inventing things, providing services that others find more difficult to do, invent or provide. These individuals and organizations have *learned* to do the *difficult* and to some extent make it routine.

To be fair, the difficulty level of something is fleeting. The Fosbury Flop, a perfect score of ten in compulsory figure skating, a triple Lutz, or multi-gigahertz processors were once difficult, but are now commonplace even to a regular/standard competitor.

So what is difficult to learn to do may be difficult only for the first learner, or for all who follow in his or her footsteps. Things that become easy to learn (or copy), those things that become commonplace, won't differentiate one actor from another, one organization from another. It's those things that *remain* elusive and hard to copy that will be seen as special or differentiating.

For each of us, difficult learning is taking on something totally new. It is deliberately putting yourself on the steepest part of the learning curve. For both individuals and organizations, *true* difficult learning is doing what someone else has never done before. This is not to be confused with not knowing how to do something – the knowledge exists, so you gather the knowledge and apply it. Difficult learning is about not knowing – because no one knows – and doing it (or attempting to do it) anyway.

A small digression – let's look at an application of difficult learning in an organizational setting. Examine Fig. 3.2.[4] Suppose you were running an organization. Where would you like the organization to be? Why? To decide we need to introduce a second concept – we'll call it value to the organization. If something (a service or product) is of high value, it can be exchanged for revenue in the marketplace. If it is of low value, whatever revenue it might be exchanged for is considerably less than in the former instance. Where would the most effective place for an organization be to sustain maximum strategic advantage? Our conclusion is that if you want to be at the top of your market, then you must be in the top right-hand category, where the usefulness of what you are doing is high, but the difficulty of learning to do and apply that strategy is also high.

Why not live an easy life in the bottom right-hand corner? Put simply, because everything that is useful and easy to do will be copied by your competitors as soon as you do it. It gives you no competitive advantage, but it does keep you in the game. This very simple chart shows a fundamental component of what is needed to lead effectively in any rapidly moving environment. It is our belief that any organization that is trying to catch up with its competitors, particularly in sectors like e-business or pharmaceuticals, will need to become good at difficult learning. In these fields, doing now what your competitors had achieved six months earlier is just not good enough. Your fastest-moving competitors will already have moved on again.

How do you learn to handle difficult learning, and how do you teach it to the rest of the organization? First, recognize that most of us were not taught to do it at school. Does that surprise you? Surely, you might argue, many of us worked hard at school, and it certainly didn't seem easy at the time! This is where we come to the crux of difficult learning and why it is, well, difficult. Difficult learning is difficult because it asks you to confront your fear of failure and fear of looking an idiot to yourself or others. Most of us have actually been taught by our school system to avoid failure, which sounds reasonable enough until we realize that the fear of that failure is what often prevents us from learning what we need to learn.

Consider this example. You are back at school and the teacher asks the class, "What is the chemical formula for sulfuric acid?" You know

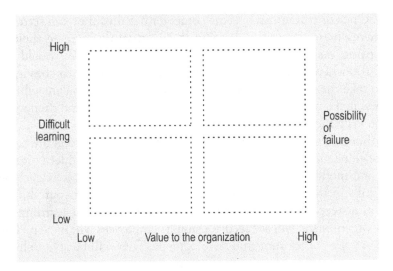

Figure 3.2 ♦ Difficult learning and competitive advantage
Source: Adapted from Hodgson, P., White, R. and Crainer, S. (1996) *The Future of Leadership*.

what will happen next. Those students who know the answer will call attention to themselves, while those who don't know will find something terribly interesting on the surface of the desk in front of them – and will do everything in their power to avoid attention. The practical learning is that when you are faced with something you don't know, you keep your head down and hope someone else deals with it. In our estimation, most children probably experience more than 10,000 episodes of this situation.

Now fast forward to that same person at work. They are faced with a difficult situation in a public arena, e.g. a senior management meeting. The chances are that they will take the same instinct that they learned at school into their organization and when faced with something they don't know, their first reaction will be to keep their head down and hope that someone else will handle it. Is this what we want in our organizations? Of course not, but we recognize that most of us – and our observations seem to apply around the world – have come through this major conditioning process at school.

It is at a fundamental level that we have to tackle fear of failure and the confidence to tackle more and more difficult learning. At schools we really want students who don't know something to jump up and shout, "I don't know, but I want to find out." Only if we fill the organizations of the future with people who are keen to explore their *lack* of knowledge will our organizations be competent at handling the things they don't know. Once organizations become competent at this, they can start making themselves competitive because they can vastly increase their rate of learning. As a teacher of social psychology put it, "We should hand you PhDs when we admit you. Then you have five years to convince us not to take them away from you." Translation: show us you are willing to explore, make mistakes, and engage in genuine learning and then we will let you keep the degree as evidence that you are truly a learner.

Although the eight factors that we describe in this chapter are considered of equal merit in handling the ambiguity that faces modern organizations and modern leaders, we do believe that the trigger for developing your skills in these areas comes from being motivated by your ability to take on a steeper learning curve and to embrace difficult learning. The future organization will succeed because its employees will have no barriers to any area of learning and development. They will be able to handle any situation and any learning opportunity.

Links with the other Enablers

Is there a clash between being motivated by mysteries and any of the other seven enablers? No, because in each of the remaining seven skills we have identified, we believe the ability to take on difficult learning is a key aspect. If you assume that the world is continually changing, and therefore greater levels of uncertainty are to be found, then the mystery not only continues, but continues to deepen.

How to be more motivated by mysteries

1. Find an old school photograph of yourself – the earlier, the better! Now gaze at the photo and try to recall what you were like then. What puzzled you? Why? What happened? How did you view mysteries in those days? What were mysteries to you? Having had a nice rummage in your long-term memory, now zoom forward to today. How could you apply some of that childlike curiosity to the issues and problems you face today? Were there incidents in your childhood that resulted in your being punished for curiosity or rewarded for a lack of it? How could you slightly modify your thinking to allow you to be more oriented toward things with an element of the unknown? Draw up a list for yourself. Choose the

least risky and the least threatening and work on it for a while. Come back after a week and review your progress. Look at the list again and discuss it with a colleague. Explore your history of being (or not being) motivated by mysteries and your current areas of mystery. Explore your colleague's areas too. What similarities and differences are there? Explore the areas of several colleagues on a business team all of you work on. How are you similar/dissimilar? Are you surprised at how alike/different you are? What does this say about your being prepared for dealing with competitors in your industry?

2. You wonder at things, but you don't explore that wonder. Your attitude is, "I don't know much about that, and I don't mind not knowing much." If a problem seems insoluble, you drop it and move on to something you can deal with. There is a Christian prayer that says, "Lord, give me the strength to handle the problems that I can do something about, the tolerance to cope with the ones I can't, and the wisdom to know the difference." You call this approach pragmatic and of course, it is. But if this attitude is also acting as a filter and preventing you from exploring unknowns that you need to know about, then it is going to be a drawback. So the next time an imponderable occurs, split it up, don't give it up. Draw up a time plan, between a week and six months long, for working on tiny, tiny areas of the imponderable. Split your elephant up into lots of bite-sized pieces, and then work on each one. If a piece is still too difficult, split it up again until you have got down to molecule-sized particles that you really can work on. After the period of time you set yourself, review where you are at. Draw two columns on a piece of paper. In the first column list the parts you have been able to do something about, and in the second column the areas where you haven't made progress. Concentrate on what you *have* been able to do, rather on what remains to be done. What did you learn from the two lists about your ability to take on something mysterious? Was there a pattern in the two lists? Incidentally, keep reminding yourself – like the dolphin – that there is no punishment in this process. All you do is to be rewarded for the progress that you have made.

3. Learn again to question. Children do it all the time. They keep asking, "Why?" "How does that work?" "What is that for?" You don't have to be quite as irritating as a young child in your use of questioning, but these questions will take you a long way in

exploring mysteries. In our experience, many managers have learned to ask questions, but then not to listen to the answers. Perhaps you have to train yourself to give your brain a pause while you really listen for the answer, even if the answer is coming from yourself. Force yourself to pause by counting slowly to five and writing down the answer someone is giving you.

4. Play the game of one to ten, which we first heard from Tim Gallwey, the author of the *Inner Game* series.[5] You have been offered coaching by two experts, both of whom know a similarly large amount about their subjects. However, before you choose which expert to work with, you discover that both experts have been asked to rate themselves on how much they know about their chosen subjects on a scale from one (low) to ten (high). One of the experts rates him/herself as an eight, the other a two. Who would you rather learn from? Well, you scored the right answer if you chose the person who rated two. Why? Given that both know a huge amount, the person who rates themselves an eight is saying, in effect, that there is not much more they could learn (especially in the known world). Whereas the person rating themselves as a two is acknowledging that although they know a huge amount already, there is an even greater amount for them to discover and learn. The more they learn, the more they realize how little they know. It's an attitude as well as knowledge. Now apply the same quiz to yourself in areas of your own expertise. Would you rather be an eight or a two? The really, really knowledgeable people in the world; i.e. those that are continually making breakthroughs into new levels of understanding, are the ones who rate themselves as a two. They recognize that they never stop exploring the boundaries of their unknown. Where on the scale are you aiming for?

5. Deliberately take on a project or task that is outside your area of expertise/competence. Choose something that is fairly low risk to start with so that you don't need to block yourself by worrying about a successful outcome. Nonetheless, try to achieve a useful outcome, and try to be sensitive to those unknown aspects of the project, which you actually find tolerable, even enjoyable. What is it that you are reacting to? What are the unknowns that are pulling you towards them? If you can understand that process, then you are well on the way to enlarging that skill at the attitude level as well as at the capability level.

6. If you can stand being near small children (and we do hope you can), then sit down and talk to some and find out what mysteries mean for them. What mysteries do they experience? Notice not only the content of what they say, but also how they convey the mystery. What attitudes are they signaling to you? With any luck, you are looking into a historical mirror. You were once like this. Use the opportunity as a stimulant for attitude memory. You can say quite truthfully, "I used to be like this." Afterwards, jot down some notes about the energy those children showed – the push of the curiosity and the pull of the unknown.

Explore and expand

- Review your attitude toward mysteries and to things that don't seem to have an obvious solution. We understand that you don't like them, but can you afford not to investigate them? Monitor your actions over the next few days, weeks, months. Can you bring the concept of the mysterious higher up your priority list?

- Try to ask "why?" more often. Just slip it into conversation and watch it do its work. Now why didn't you think of that?

- Find a colleague who seems more of a Mystery-Seeker than you are. Work jointly on a shared project. How did the colleague approach the unknown? How did you? What kinds of questions did each of you ask?

Notes

1. The *Ambiguity Architect™: Navigating Rough Water* is available from Lominger Limited, Inc., Minneapolis, MN. Visit their website at www.performanceprograms.com.

2. Crainer, S. and Dearlove, D. (2000) *Generation Entrepreneur.* London: ft.com.

3. Angus Maddison, IMF. *The Economist,* December 31 1999.

4. White, R., Hodgson, P., and Crainer, S. (1996) *The Future of Leadership: Riding the Corporate Rapids into the 21st Century* London: Pitman Publishing, p. 151.

5. Gallwey, W. T. (1997) *The Inner Game of Tennis.* New York: Random House.

ENABLER 2

BE RISK TOLERANT

Being on the tightrope is living; everything else is waiting.
Karl Wallenda (1904–78)

What is risk?

The word *risk* has become so widely used that it tends to mean almost anything that is unknown. Mark Haynes Daniell offers the following four-stage systematic definition of risk:

- the scale of the potential harm – adjusted by
- the likelihood of that harm occurring – net of
- the ability of an effective response to be put in place – adjusted by
- the likelihood of that response mechanism being deployed effectively.[6]

This is a definition based on modern financial and economic thinking, and even here at each stage there is uncertainty. But what if you are trying to go outside the bounds of economic analysis and explore behavior and skills?

In terms of understanding the skill of risk tolerance, the person who is tolerant of a risk must know that there is a risk in the first place. There is a comparison here to courage. To be truly courageous you must know that there is danger. If you are unaware of the danger, are you really being courageous? Similarly, if a person is unaware of the risk in their action, then they are not being tolerant of the risk itself. To some extent the assessment of danger, like that for risk, is in the eye of the beholder. What looks risky to me may be nothing to you. If you are prepared to take a chance and make a decision when aware of the risk, you are probably a **Risk-Tolerator**.

Different societies around the world seem to have varying levels of tolerance for risk. In many ways it can be argued that the Western world has become less risk tolerant. Legislation, and particularly litigation, have been used to reduce risk and to reduce a citizen's individual liability for understanding, managing, and tolerating the outcome of risk. Famous court cases in the US, such as the "hot coffee incident" at McDonald's (where a person ordered coffee from the drive-through counter, subsequently spilled it on her legs causing severe scalding, and successfully sued McDonald's for selling her a dangerous product) demonstrate that individual citizens are apparently not prepared to acknowledge that there is a risk of burning themselves if they handle hot coffee in a car.

Perversely, however, there seems to be an increase in some people's interest in and preference for activities, particularly leisure activities, that include greater levels of risk. It wasn't that many years ago that bungee jumpers were only known on a few islands in the west Pacific; now it seems to be a commonplace activity. Equally, the increase in white-knuckle rides at amusement parks suggests a public demand for a feeling of risk without the actual taking of the risk. Risk has become an "experience" we seek and are even prepared to pay for. Perhaps this is because our lives are now free of real personal risk. There are many people who gamble, spending vast amounts of money at games of chance and in lotteries supposedly because they have nothing to lose. It suggests to us that many humans need some degree of risk to have "fun," yet individuals are tolerant of different levels of perceived risk. The progress of civilization through history seems to be about reducing the real risks involved in survival. A society describes itself as more civilized when it is facing fewer risks to its present and future.

Given these different perspectives on risk, what we are referring to when we use the phrase risk tolerant is where the probability of something going wrong stemming from a particular action or decision is known to the person who is taking the risk. They may not be aware of the actual statistical probability of the occurrence of a negative event, but they must be aware there is a potential downside to the decision or action they are taking or asking others to take. When Fred Smith of FedEx gambled at Las Vegas and won (so that he could make the payroll that month), he knew that the downside was, if not the closure of his business, then at least a severe dent in the vision he had for his fledgling business.[7] The obvious trend of more decisions being made in a shorter time cycle brings with it another range of business risks. It is ironic that, in what Steve Case (CEO of AOL/Time Warner) has dubbed the internet century, organizations find themselves more frequently facing either zero information or vast overloads of information.[8] In a world of limited information, intuition is very important because to make the *right* decision based on little or no information could put you well ahead of your competitors. In a world with too much information, intuition is equally important, since there's probably no way that you can go through the data and still make a timely decision. It seems to us that many managers are having to use information differently and more intuitively than even a few years ago.

Risk-Tolerators are ...

Risk-Tolerators can make decisions when necessary despite incomplete information and will tolerate the risk of failure. They are not hampered by insufficient or ambiguous data.

Signs of Risk-Tolerators

Tell-tale signs

- Understand the timing of decisions. Gerstner, IBM's CEO, knew that IBM's future was more important than an early decision.

- Understand possible risks of the decision or lack of decision.

- Probably attracted to doing things that are new – so there is a link to Motivated by Mysteries.

- See a hierarchy of risk. For example, Russia's president Vladimir Putin moved his approval rating from rock bottom to a comfortable majority in late 1999 by taking the risk of promoting the war in Chechnya, even though generally people don't like conscript wars.

- Can be intuitive – for example, Albert Einstein wondering what it would be like to ride around the galaxy on the front of a light beam or Walt Disney acting out the parts of each of the cartoon characters, complete with voices.

Tell-tale actions

- Make decisions when the decision needs to be made without full information, but are not impetuous.

- See risk as a route to increasing experience, knowledge, and opportunity.

- Think through and accept the consequences of failure or of some outcome not forecast.

- Make decisions in the face of contrary conventional views – for example, Richard Branson starting an Atlantic airline in the face of major competitors.

- Shift gears to handle several levels of risk. In other words, a risk taken now may prevent a larger risk later.

Tell-tale phrases

- "I know we don't know, but we still need to decide."

- "It's never been done before – that's what makes it attractive."

- "Let's grab that opportunity, even though we don't know the details."

- "I have learned to live with the consequences of my colleagues' actions."

Case study

The case of the risky recruit

Sheila runs the management development group based in the head office of a major European manufacturing organization. She has always been a bit of a renegade. As the result of some domestic upheaval when she was a teenager, and although she was very bright, she pulled out of school at the earliest legal age. On the strength of an address sent by postcard from a school friend now working in Italy, she traveled across Europe by herself to seek out her friend, settled in Italy, and then traveled around the rest of Europe.

She had lots of adventures in Europe, and briefly in America, and arrived back home at the age of 23 with lots of experience but no prospects. She took herself back to school to finish off her secondary education, then took an undergraduate degree and then a Master's. She saw nothing unusual in educating herself in this way. As she said, "I didn't have a personality to educate until I'd traveled around and found who I really was." Her persistence and motivation to challenge, and thus to take major risks with her prospects, were indicative of the person.

She worked in two or three organizations in various roles for the following five years and then got a job with her present employer. The interview process was to last one and a half days, starting Tuesday afternoon with the first interview, followed by a plant tour on Wednesday morning, and the final interview on Wednesday afternoon.

In the Tuesday interview the visiting HR manager from a nearby research division challenged an assertion she had made regarding his shift workers and their keenness on self-managed development. They argued as best they could at the time, but it was unresolved. After all, he had all the data and he knew the people. She didn't appear on Wednesday morning until halfway through the plant visit, and although nothing was said by the company, it was clearly odd behavior and not likely to improve her chances. Everyone assumed that a black mark had been allocated to her. The reason she didn't appear was that she spent part of the night before on the phone to the research division. She contacted and interviewed 15 of the very nightshift workers whose motivation she had been discussing with the HR manager earlier. It took half the morning to compile her report, so of course she was late for the plant visit. She presented the report at the final board meeting to the astounded HR manager to justify her assertion on the previous day. The board liked her, and her tolerance for risk. They recognized they were dealing with someone different and special and acknowledged that this organization had until now been good at minimizing and avoiding risk. They decided to take her on. She started in a training role, then moved to a wider management development role.

Despite at times lack of board support, she has seized one opportunity after another using her intellect and social skills to push her own and others' ideas into operation. Typically her method is to implement the idea on a small scale, then to use the positive results to bludgeon proper funding and support for a larger-scale implementation.

She works quickly and fluidly, often appearing to want to conduct two or three conversations at a time and hardly ever finishing a sentence or a meeting completely. Her people say she is very open about the risks that she and they are taking, but never fails to emphasize the rewards that are in reach. Although there is some undoubted bravado in her style, which is not to everyone's taste, she is very pragmatic about the negative face of the risks she takes.

She always wants to know what the risks are – she calls it "looking into the abyss." Where the risk seems great, or more precisely the consequences of failure are dramatic, she will put a lot of effort into ensuring that there is a fail-safe option, so that the risk will have moved the company along in some way. Her people say that the post-event reviews she always carries out are extremely rigorous but positive. Even if the whole project has been a disaster, there is still a positive outcome and positive learning to be gained from it, and she emphasizes that to everyone associated. In the reviews, everybody faces up to what worked and what didn't work, and everybody comes out having learned a lot more about the task they were trying to achieve and often about themselves, too.

What happens if no one wants to tolerate risk?

We mentioned the dramatic decline of *Encyclopaedia Britannica* (p. 43) and wondered how things might have turned out if a senior manager had been motivated by mysteries. But if that curiosity had not been bolstered by a readiness to take and tolerate risk, we doubt that any serious action would have resulted. When your product has been successful for more than two and a half centuries when sold as weighty tomes, it will seem like a huge risk to convert it to a few thin, insubstantial silvery disks, and soon after that to online servers where the perceived value is diminished by free alternatives like Wikipedia. The directors of *Britannica* were not prepared to take a risk in understanding that they were not a publisher of books, but they were a conveyer and seller of knowledge. And that the new medium that was going to take over a huge proportion of knowledge transfer and storage was going to be electronic and digital not paper and ink.

Now ask yourself this question. Is something like this happening in your organization? To what extent are you prepared to take the risk to explore, to learn, and possibly to fail? How much are you deliberately taking risks in order that you might move forward some steps on a yet unrecognized game board? A veteran of a firm now free-falling out of the

Fortune 500 is quoted as having said, "The clue train stopped there four times a day for ten years and they never took delivery."[9]

If Sheila hadn't been prepared to take the risk of arriving late at the plant visit, it's doubtful she would have been offered the job. Equally, in her current job, part of her role is to tolerate risks that other more senior and staid members of her organization are not prepared to face. Without risk, the result would be an organization that had far fewer opportunities both individual and organizational development initiatives.

Organizations that are not risk tolerant will stifle themselves in the search for more data, when probably that data is never going to be available or certainly not available in a time scale that would make sense in a business context. Organizations often drown in the data that they have accumulated and soon that accumulation of data is getting in the way of making clear and rapid decisions. The more data that accumulates, the slower the rate of decision making and the less learning that occurs in a particular time frame. (For example, Ford and Firestone were skewered for having data on defective tires that was two years old before anyone voiced concern or was courageous enough to take a risk!)

> Organizations that can't face up to risks cannot shift gears easily.

Organizations need to prepare to leave existing areas of comfort and move into new areas that might produce new opportunities and new products. For example, the Xerox process did not come from the printing industry; the electric typewriter did not come from a typewriter manufacturer; the personal computer was not originated by a major mainframe computer manufacturer; instant film was not made by the major film makers. There is a pattern in innovation in the twenty-first century. Many of the new products have not come from the industries where that product represented a development or an extension of an existing product. Organizations that can't face up to risks cannot shift gears easily. They spend too long on the threat of an unlikely risk and probably not enough time on understanding a real threat. For instance, Barnes and Noble very effectively fought off other booksellers through better buildings, designs, location, etc. But that did not help them recognize the internet as a potential competitor to traditional books or the phenomenal success of Amazon. Contrast them with Microsoft, which, while originally slow to appreciate the internet, was extremely fast (some say less than a month) in turning around and adjusting their work efforts to focus on the internet and its opportunities.

Links with other Enablers

Part of the ability to tolerate risk is to know that if the worst outcome happens you can still survive or at least do something about it. This suggests to us that the ability to look ahead, and particularly the futurist aspect of this, will prepare you for anticipating when risks might turn sour (*see* p. 62). Equally, the ability to be flexible when things get difficult gives you the chance to handle the outcome of a badly taken risk more competently (*see* p. 93). Finally, recognizing that you won't know if it's a risk if you're overly focused may persuade you to lift your head up from time to time and look at the wider picture (*see* p. 115).

How to be more risk tolerant

1. Think of a decision (one that turned out well) that you have taken part in recently and list on a sheet of paper all of the data that you felt might be necessary to effectively make the decision. Now with the benefit of hindsight, look back on what the minimum data could have been to make that decision. Rework the analysis one more time and say, "If I could only have had access to 60 percent of the minimum, which 60 percent would have given me the strongest clue as to what the right decision turned out to be?"

2. Once you have proven to yourself with some analysis of past positive outcomes that not all data is necessary, try something for real. Choose a decision that you are going to have to make, but let's not go losing sleep over this one, so choose a decision that isn't too important. You'd normally ask for some data on this, wouldn't you? On this decision, ask for far less data – in fact, push your luck a little bit and, learning from the previous example, ask for 60 percent of the minimum data that you'd normally expect. Now make the decision. Yes, that's right go ahead and just do it. Ask yourself, "How do I feel?" and jot your feelings down in a private note to yourself. A week or so later (or whenever the outcome of your decision is known) ask, "Did it work or did it flop?" Also ask yourself the same question, "How do I feel?" Review your feelings and learning from this experiment. What is it that makes you feel more comfortable working with less data? What are the aspects that made you feel least comfortable?

3. Now we come to the advanced level. Make a decision purely on gut instinct. Take it easy the first time – we don't want to be responsible for increased blood pressure, stress or any of the other afflictions of corporate life – but go on, make a decision. Use the same method as before to review your feelings. Over a period of time, try more than one decision by gut instinct. Can you start to make some distinctions between a decision that you are prepared to make more comfortably (we didn't say you'd be completely comfortable) and a decision that just seems impossible to make without a full analysis? Based on this analysis, where can you improve in your work? Because gut instinct and intuition are a faster way of gathering data and making decisions, how could you speed up your work with the knowledge you have gained from this exercise?

4. Work with someone who seems more tolerant of risk than yourself. Explore both their methods and their feelings. Ask them why they do what they do as well as how they do it. Is it bravado that they seem to not worry about the risk? Are they aware of the risk in the same way you are? Do they see risk as fitting into a longer-term strategy for which they have some kind of fail-safe response?

5. Look back on previous mistakes that seemed crushing at the time. How much impact did they really have on your business or career?

6. On a day when you have many meetings, each requiring decisions to be made on your part or on your group's part, be prepared to chart the following: What was the situation? What decision did you make or did you help the group make? What was your role in decision making? What was your behavior like? How do you feel about the outcome? Now look back on the day – how easily did you move from decision to decision, meeting to meeting? Did you use the same behavior all day? (Did you need copious amounts of facts and figures, or were you unable to make a decision?) Did you find it difficult to transition your behavior, or did you easily shift from one decision to another? Ask others who were with you in multiple meetings about their impressions of your behavior. If you and they believe you transition easily from one decision to another, you shift gears easily. If you and they didn't see this, then here is an area to explore.

Most of us have a consistent set of behaviors we try to utilize, but this can sometimes blind us to the situational nature of the response that is required of us – too hard, too controlling, needing too much data can be just the right set of behaviors or just the wrong set depending on the riskiness of the situation. Effectiveness requires a range of these behaviors, even in the same meeting!

Explore and expand

- Take small risks and small steps. If you aren't comfortable with risk, then don't frighten yourself even further. It's fine to go for even the smallest, lowest, least risky options as long as it's an increase on what you currently do.

- Review immediately, but also over a longer period. A risk may seem much greater at first than it does even a few weeks or a few months later. Learn something about the way that the passing of time affects the level of perceived risk.

- Look at a time when you tried something and failed. What was the situation? What did you learn? What have been the consequences on you, your family, your career? Make time to list positive as well as any negative consequences.

- As risk is in the eye of the beholder to some extent, find out what you see as risky and compare that with what others see as risky. It's quite possible that in some other people's eyes, you are seen as more risk tolerant than they are. Wouldn't that be fun?

Notes

6. Daniell, M.H. (2000) *World of Risk: Next Generation Strategy for a Volatile Era*. New York: John Wiley & Sons, p. 11.

7. Wetherbe, J. (1996) *The World on Time: The 11 Management Principles that Made Fedex an Overnight Sensation*. Knowledge Exchange.

8. Gunther, M. (2000) "These guys want it all," in *Fortune*, 7 February, pp. 29–33.

9. Locke, C. and Levine, R. (2000) *The Cluetrain Manifesto*. London: ft.com.

ENABLER 3

SCAN AHEAD

Research is what I'm doing when I don't know what I'm doing.

Wernher von Braun (1912–77)

Polish up your personal radar

"Who knows what tomorrow may bring?" goes the old folk song, and the answer we found is that no one knows. But according to our research, less than half of the managers we studied seemed any better than the mythical "typical" manager at preparing themselves and their organizations for what might happen next. They are **Future-Scanners**.

Future-Scanners link two skills. They are futurists – gazing into the future and imagining the possibilities of an idea, invention, product, service, and they 'drill deep' – being curious and intent on asking the right questions at the right time, even in areas where they lack detailed or technical knowledge. Incidentally, have you ever noticed that the best general managers are always able to ask the penetrating questions – the ones that get right to the heart of the matter, even in areas they appear to know little about? These are people who recognize that in a world of complex information overload, their ability to seize on even the faintest signals of what the future might become and explore its possibilities will have an essential competitive advantage. We know of one top manager who during presentations from members of his division hardly ever hears the whole presentation through before butting in with questions like, "So what are you going to do about X?" or "So how is that going to help you handle Y?" His staff acknowledge that sometimes it is a little irritating, but they are often agog with the depth of his perception and the quality of the questions that he can ask when newly presented with a myriad of data. It's not lost on us that the addition of some people-valuing skills wouldn't hurt either.

> Future-Scanners link two skills. They are futurists and they "drill deep."

Future-Scanners are curious and inquisitive. They tend to ask lots of penetrating questions. They have command of interesting facts, figures, and hunches. They also, much like Lew Frankfort of Coach, the leather goods maker, tend to raise questions or frame questions that others haven't thought of before. In Lew's case, Coach made high-fashion leather containers – bags, handbags, purses, wallets, etc. Lew realized that the skills his people possessed with leather could be used on a far wider range of products. He wouldn't stand for the "we're a bag maker" approach. In a series of boundary-pushing conversations first with his staff, then with potential customers, Lew stimulated a much wider range of options for their leather-working skills. Because of Lew's questioning, Lexus cars started using Coach-branded leather seats.

Future-Scanners also have a tendency to make connections between apparently disparate areas. They then have the ability to parlay them into a marketable/saleable product or a conclusion about the data that others don't reach. Sir Arthur Conan Doyle created the detective, Sherlock Holmes, who had the uncanny knack of probing deeply for the data that was available, but was also acutely aware of the unlikely and the unusual. He showed an ability to understand the logic of the situation to a greater depth than his friend and sidekick Dr Watson. His intuition even allowed him to know when some data was missing and why its absence was significant.

Inspector Gregory: Is there any other point to which you would wish to draw my attention?
Holmes: To the curious incident of the dog in the night-time.
Inspector Gregory: The dog did nothing in the night-time.
Holmes: That was the curious incident.

To discover the importance of the dog not barking, read Doyle, A.C. (1930) 'The Adventure of Silver Blaze,' in *Memoirs of Sherlock Holmes*, Doubleday.[10] Without question, these skills are required for any new enterprise to go forward. They are also required for good fiction – the story has to be believable and attractive. We sometimes wonder if good science fiction and good business development in an area like the internet might actually look very similar.

Future-Scanners are ...

Future-Scanners have the ability to question deeply and make links between apparently different pieces of information, while being constantly on the lookout for even the faintest signals of what the future might hold.

Signs of Future-Scanners

We have sub-divided Future-Scanners into two categories, "futurists" and "deep drillers."

Futurists

Tell-tale signs

- Are always preparing for possibilities.
- Are different from the mainstream scenario composers by allowing themselves to be available to propositions about the future that may be odd or extreme.
- Have ideas that may not fit into current thinking.
- Are attracted to ideas that may be dismissed by most people.

Tell-tale actions

- Reach out into the future for ideas, information, or hunches.
- Display a kind of predictive intuition.
- Explore possibilities by linking together apparently unconnected future ideas.
- Listen constantly for "faint signals" of what may become significant.

Tell-tale phrases

- "That's a great idea."
- "I wonder if we could develop that?"

- "What would happen if this were to occur under those circumstances?"
- "We need to be ready to exploit that opportunity even though it is unlikely."
- "How would it be if we could ...?"
- "What if we could ...?"

Deep drillers

Tell-tale signs

- Want to know how things work.
- Want to get a grip on how things will work out.
- Want to understand the "core of the process."
- Are prepared to take a long time to really understand how things work in the organization.
- People say about their style of inquiry, "Why didn't I think of asking that?"
- Are curious about the "system underneath the surface."
- Are interested in propositions about facts and data and the logic that connects them.

Tell-tale actions

- Explore the logic of the situation so they can hone in on the key facts.
- Question and pull together key pieces of the argument to see the essential data and where data is missing.
- Seek a more fundamental understanding of the world.

Tell-tale phrases

- "What are the implications of that action? And what are the unintended consequences?"

- "How does this information link with that information?"
- "What is missing in our understanding of this?"
- "What would we like to know if we could find it out?"
- "Why does it have to happen this way?"

Case study

The case of the battered business plan

My first introduction to Stevie was seeing an angry member of her staff burst out of the conference room shouting to no one in particular, "That woman is so annoying!" The door, left slightly ajar, showed a room that might have been discovered after a major earthquake. Cups, chairs, tables, papers, computers, people strewn around as if flung by a giant hand. I met the owner of the (metaphorical) hand a moment later. Stevie was sitting, leaning back in her chair, somehow managing to look intense and serene all at the same time. She was holding a major review meeting with the heads of the division she had taken over just six months previously to present their proposed business plans. When I joined them, they had reached the all-important discussion and presentation of web page designs.

This meeting wasn't a relaxed affair. This was the first chance for the department heads to stretch themselves. The entire future of the organization depended on first-rate decisions coming from this meeting – and deadlines weren't too far away. Stevie had seen an advanced draft business plan and had realized that while they were reasonably ambitious based on what the division had done before, they also showed a narrowness of vision. There was a lack of understanding of how the output of this division – basically a technical software function – could be linked to the more customer-facing divisions to produce a heart-stopping product. Stevie knew less about the division than the managers she was sitting with, so she had to use part of the time in the meeting to learn what they thought was really possible. But she had to help them see a wider image and a wider range of possibilities. She could tell them, of course, but that wouldn't recruit them to working on it for themselves. She had to prove to them that there was a better and bigger way.

During the next hour Stevie questioned her colleagues deeply about various aspects of the plans and designs. She was relentless in pushing for all the pieces to "add up," not just at the surface, but also at deeper levels. She not only wanted the new proposals to be and look good, but they must link back to past products. Customers and competitors would see an unbroken stream of ideas and concepts from past through present to future. Although Stevie did around 50 percent of the questioning, she always encouraged her team to use her own approach on everyone in the room, including herself. And she was not immune to having her ideas put in front of the pressure hose. A feature of their conversation was that at one moment tiny details – like the look of a screen icon – were being discussed intently, and the next moment the biggest of big pictures was in the room – where our industry will be in three, five, ten, 100 years. Future-Scanners like Stevie seem to be able to flick effortlessly from the minute to the major according to the needs of the conversation.

What was outstanding about Stevie's ability was not only that she questioned and pressed for the logic and the data to make sense, but she was also able to bring little snippets of data from all kinds of sources into the existing conversation. A proposal for a new screen icon was improved by referring to an illustration she'd seen on a recent trip to India. A reference to a piece of design brought a link with a comment she had heard from a computer design engineer at Boeing. A screen color brought a reference to a new textile product from Courtaulds. Always links, always options, always additional information that might just contribute to a more intriguing future.

Yes, it was frustrating to work with Stevie. Good ideas that people had put a lot of effort into could still get mangled if they were unable to survive the rigor of the tough questioning process that Stevie encouraged. Those ideas didn't just have to survive the questioning, they also had to line up with her and her colleagues' understanding of what was going to be needed next. But although frustrating, the process was highly infectious and very absorbing. Just 15 minutes after her outburst against the boss, the staff member I'd first seen storming out of the meeting was back in there pitching, linking and generating a new future with the rest of the team.

What happens if no one scans ahead?

Can you imagine starting up a new business with a great entrepreneurial idea and not having any sense of how things might turn out? The ability to scan ahead seems to be most needed when starting something new or modifying something extensively.

How long would you give the organization whose best efforts at new products were simply changing the color, repackaging or putting on a flash branding that said the word "new?" Wouldn't you be more attracted to products and services that seemed to anticipate your changing needs and that tried to meet your needs or even create alternative ones rather than staying with the past? But we'd guess that you'd not want new for the sake of new. Whatever it is has to be coherent, match your needs, and make sense for the future. The original digital watches were heavy and required two hands to operate compared to their analogue rivals. Rightly, they didn't last long. In the same way, we wonder how much longer PC users will tolerate having to press "control, alt and delete," to get the errant machines back under control?

If Stevie had not been able to explore the logic of the plans presented to her by drilling deep and also to offer new aspects, new information and new possibilities to her divisional team, she would almost certainly have had to resort to telling them what to do. No doubt they would have tried their best, but without really understanding the perspective she had, they would never be able to implement it to its full potential. That meeting was crucial not only because of the decisions eventually made and agreed on, but because of the breadth of understanding that the other divisional vice-presidents emerged with by the end of what became known as the "battered business plan day."

Where's the vision?

Sometimes we are asked if scanning ahead is the same as vision. Our answer is, "It depends." Our experience of the use of vision and the process of visioning in organizations is that this word can have one of two meanings.

- **Meaning 1** The vision is a social construction of reality made in the present and, as often as not, a contradiction of the likely trends of the future. It is essentially a device to create the possibility of a new and different future that is deliberately different from what might otherwise happen. In this sense it can serve as an inspiring message to followers. In extreme cases, it is a revolutionary tool. The classic "I have a dream" speech of Martin Luther King Jr was a vision in the face of the likely future reality that most people at that time believed would happen.[11] Because the overall purpose of this kind of vision is to change the world, then this meaning of the term goes far beyond what we are describing here as scanning ahead. Scanning ahead is understanding and preparing for the *likely* future, whatever that might be. Visioning in this context is about driving through to a new future, and of course the vision may not change, even though the circumstances do.

- **Meaning 2** If the vision is a projection of where we think we will be if we continue down these particular pathways and apply the current strategies, then it is used in a very similar meaning to our expression, scanning ahead.

How to enhance your future-scanning

The futurist

1. Note down five things that you feel will influence your business or the way you do business over the next ten years. Compare your notes with someone to see what they have put down. If you have professional futurists in your organization, go and talk to them and ask what kinds of things they are concerned about. Your aim is to increase your day-to-day awareness of situations and events in your future that might affect how you do your job and how your organization does what.

2. Get hold of an article by a futurist writer (e.g. Michio Kaku) or read some classic science fiction (like something by Arthur C. Clarke). How does your list above compare with theirs?

3. Think back to five years ago. Read old business plans, statements about the future, any kind of predictive material – particularly if you were involved in writing it – and see how accurately it worked out. What can you learn from reviewing this (apart from being careful with what you write in the future)? In future (literally and figuratively) meetings, start more sentences with the phrase "What if we could ...?" Chart the impact on yourself and your colleagues of the questions you've asked and the answers you get. How future-oriented are your colleagues? How can you help them become more so? Don't forget that the easiest way to learn something is to teach someone else.

Deep drillers

1. We recommended using the question "why?" as a kind of side-arm for Future-Scanners. People who are drilling deep also use the word "why," but they qualify it. So try using the question "Why does it have to happen this way?" They also use the word "how" as in "How does X link with Y?" or "How does this information fit in with what you previously told me?" Try using these questions and watch the response you get.

2. Draw up a consequence chart. This is where you begin with the end outcome of some activity. For instance, you win a new order from a valued customer then chart back the actions that led to that success. Make a chain of these actions. Now using the same technique, start at the other end of the time scale with something quite trivial. For instance, your computer crashes and you fail to receive an e-mail from a colleague, which means you head off to the airport not knowing that the deal has changed, and you arrive at the customer's office unaware of the shift in attitude, and the business deal is lost. Look at how the consequences from even a small incident can have quite major positive or negative outcomes. Draw some consequence charts for both positive and negative outcomes of recent projects you have been involved in. What do you learn about the linkages between what was discussed and what was intended? What data was used and what were the real outcomes?

Explore and expand

*   Build some time into your schedule for the future. Yes, we know it sounds strange, but make thinking about the future a task. If it's easier, trade ideas with colleagues and stretch your mind a little bit into the future. For managers in most organizations, it's all too easy to be completely focused on the present.

*   Talk to people outside your business – teenagers, for instance. They will have made assumptions about their immediate future without realizing they are making predictions. Ask them what they see in their world and compare it with your perceptions.

- With apologies to the old Hewlett-Packard commercial, use the phrase "what if?" as often as possible. "What if we did that?" "What if this happened?" "What if we could meet this requirement?" Don't use it as your only phrase, but get it into the conversation more often and watch the result both on others and yourself.

- And of course, review, review, review! What have you learned?

Notes

10. For the rest of the story read "The Adventure of Silver Blaze" to discover the importance of the dog not barking; we won't spoil it for you.

11. King, Martin Luther Jr (1963) *I Have a Dream*. Address at Lincoln Memorial, Washington, DC, August 28.

ENABLER 4

TACKLE TOUGH ISSUES

I have not failed. I've just found 10,000 ways that won't work.

Thomas Edison (1847–1931)

It isn't interesting if it isn't challenging

John Harrison (the inventor of the first chronometer, which allowed longitude to be accurately measured by ships at sea) followed doggedly the pursuit of more accurate time-keeping mechanisms for over 50 years. Harrison expected to win the £20,000 prize (today worth several million dollars) offered by the British Parliament in the Longitude Act (1714) for the first determination of longitude for ships at sea, accurate to half a degree. Despite enormous political opposition, obfuscation, and general political low dealing, Harrison kept at the development of his clock and watch mechanisms and at chipping away at successive versions of the government. Eventually, he got his reward by appealing directly to King George III.

It was said of one British cabinet minister that he would cross the road to join a fight. **Tenacious Challengers** don't spend their entire lives fighting, although to some of their colleagues it might seem that way, but they do love a challenge, either in the assignments they take on or in their pursuit of an objective. Fredy Dellis, when CEO of the car rental firm Europcar in the early 1990s, saw that among many problems the cost per transaction at Europcar was 12 or 13 times as great as at its rivals Avis and Hertz. Following the logical trail of implications from that one fact translated into the need to take a huge risk by installing a Europe-wide integrated IT system.[12] Tenacious Challengers are motivated when they are told that something can't be done or has never been tried before because no one thought it possible. If something is very difficult and has been attempted but never achieved, then the Tenacious Challenger is at the front of the line to get on and have a go at it themselves.

Sir Ranulph Fiennes, the polar explorer, imagines himself to be escaping from the Russian Gulag when he is walking across the polar icecap so that every step takes him further away from his misery.[13] His greatest concern is what he calls the "whining voice" inside himself, where every step he takes, things get worse not better. Tenacious Challengers keep on working at things – they won't let anything go. They won't let whining voices get in the way. They just keep plugging away at it until they finally find a route through or bring together the right people to make the right solution.

> Tenacious Challengers keep on working at things – they won't let anything go.

Tenacious Challengers are in it for the long term. It took the late Gene Cattabiani, former EVP of Westinghouse Power Generation, years and five special board presentations to sell his management colleagues on the importance of merging critical parts of the steam turbine business. In addition, he was prescient enough to move them to a neutral site in the hope of ensuring the integration necessary for success. He fought, argued, and cajoled because it would cost millions, and others didn't share his view of the necessity to combine these critical parts of what many said was a dying business. In the end, with the increased productivity, he was able to repay the corporation in five years with the synergy from the move.

We heard of an organization that pursued a potential customer for more than seven years before that customer bought anything. Within the organization there must have been people who were saying, "Enough is enough – let's look elsewhere," but that customer is now one of the single largest sources of revenue for the organization. Tenacious Challengers tend to ignore the easier assignments in the organizational world and are uniquely drawn to the tough ones. There's a difference here between an unknown assignment that motivates the Mystery-Seeker, and a tough assignment that motivates the Tenacious Challenger. The assignment is tough because other people have tried to do this particular work and have failed – or at least not succeeded as robustly as was hoped. Like Christie's Inspector Poirot or Conan Doyle's Sherlock Holmes, a seemingly unlikely item or clue can be of just as much interest as the obvious.

One of the managing directors of three partially merged healthcare organizations tenaciously stuck to the theme of creating a common external phone number for all inquiries to any of the three organizations. It was a relatively trivial service and one regarded as unimportant by other colleagues. But he knew that as long as the three organizations presented themselves to the world as three separate institutions with three separate phone numbers, none of the internal staff would believe and behave as if those three organizations could really operate as one. His long-term insistence eventually led to a much more integrated organization.

Tenacious Challengers know that they are going to face many setbacks and many unforeseen problems on the way, but they have a built-in sense of determination and perseverance that allows them to keep going when other people have decided it is not worth the effort. In 1985 when Intel decided to get out of memory chips, they had to reduce staffing levels by 30 percent. They threw themselves from having a certain but modest future into a place where only the toughest would survive. Aside from Intel, any number of inventors – from Westinghouse and Ford to Jobs and Watt – and their successful inventions, are the direct result of being/acting as challengers. Think exploding the status quo and you find challenger.

But there can be a dark side to this skill. When overdone and overused, the Tenacious Challenger may seem obsessive and perhaps even blind to outside influences. Brian Swette, the former EVP and chief marketing officer of Pepsi-Cola, described himself thus: "My life is one-dimensional. Work and then more work. But we're doing something important – creating a legacy."[14] He is now COO for eBay, where incidentally in February 2000 his stock options were valued at $242,000,000! Imagine working for or with Brian if you didn't share his dream or passion to make eBay a leading trading site on the internet?

Tenacious Challengers are ...

Tenacious Challengers resolutely pursue difficult and challenging issues and problems. This skill is most often seen in inventors and start-up artists, and is sometimes perceived as the entrepreneurial part of entrepreneurs. They are at home with conflict.

Signs of Tenacious Challengers

We have sub-divided Tenacious Challengers into "motivated by challenge" and "tenacious."

Motivated by challenge

Tell-tale signs

- Confidence isn't the issue here. Some people are, some are less so. The issue is a dogged determination to make something happen.
- When the going gets tough, the motivation increases.
- Understand that the best solutions to a problem give every stakeholder a share of the winnings.
- Recognize that organizations have multiple objectives and executives often face conflicting tasks and objectives.
- Are sometimes suspected by others of creating turbulence where none needs to exist.

Tell-tale actions

- Seek out the difficult.
- Welcome the complexity of the problem.
- Face up to difficult choices in fixing or developing a business.

Tell-tale phrases

- "It wouldn't be interesting if it wasn't difficult."
- "It's a great challenge."
- "We've got to find a better way."

Tenacious

Tell-tale signs

- When overdone can appear to be obsessive, unthinking, and unrealistic.
- Really do view every problem as an opportunity.

Tell-tale actions

- Keep going despite wavering or little support from others.

- Doggedly pursue their objective no matter what.

- See *new* possibilities and opportunities in current problems and difficulties, and use these possibilities as sources of energy and encouragement.

- Puzzle over an issue or apparent contradiction to follow the trail.

Tell-tale phrases

- "We have to keep going."

- "We'll get there."

- "We all have setbacks – that doesn't matter."

Case study

The case of the chief executive's unmentionables

If I didn't know better, I'd think he was always trying to test himself in some way. It isn't that he picks fights – although in this firm he is no stranger to controversy – it's just that he seems to be attracted by every difficult issue or situation. Every organization has its unmentionables, you know, the things and issues that we all know are there but no one has tackled because no one can see an easy or at least a clear solution. (The speaker, a long-serving executive, was describing his current CEO.)

Before John arrived, the previous CEO had been sitting on three problems. The finance director used to be good, but he had lost his edge – nothing too obvious, but he was only just keeping up, definitely not leading the pack. Then there was the chain of dealers who were resting on their laurels. Because they were based in some of the most lucrative areas, their sales still looked good compared with many other regions. Everyone knew it would take a lot of effort to set up a rival dealership. And of course, there was the overlap between two of their most competent researchers in the newly merged research facility. No one wanted to tackle the issue of who was going to lose their budget with these very good and conscientious people, for fear they might lose them both.

When John arrived, he discovered these problems existed and immediately set about taking some action to get something done about each one. They now have a new finance director and a much invigorated and shaken up dealer chain. The research group is midway through a review of their overall strategy and purpose, but the results look good and they are hopeful that they will not lose any of their best researchers.

John always seems to revel in these imponderable and difficult problems. He wades in and keeps working at them until there is a solution. It often isn't a very elegant solution, but he gets something done, and nine times out of ten the company is better off as a result of what he has achieved.

John doesn't stop when the trail goes cold. After the last round of acquisitions and mergers, there was a fiendishly complex situation related to long-term agreements over the ownership and distribution of certain global brands. Any number of players and interest groups were involved, including three main board directors who had each worked on some of those brands themselves in earlier parts of their careers.

It was a core problem that a number of other directors had looked at and then backed off. It seemed to involve so many senior people and so much of their history. Who wanted to fall out with at least 51 percent of the strong people in the firm by tackling something that no one would thank you for solving? But John realized that if this question was not resolved, then a central plank of the integration of the organization would never be put in place. If the organization was going to move on and think of itself in a new and more nimble light, it had to be integrated around the issues raised by the distribution of these particular global brands. It must have cost him a lot of energy and certainly tested some of his friendships, or at least his relationships with key managers. But John kept at it until he found resolutions to the issues and got things sorted out. Everyone else in the company heaved a great sign of relief when he did. No one else had wanted to volunteer to tackle the issues in the first place, yet everyone knew they needed to be tackled.

What happens when no one wants to tackle tough issues?

Things drift. From the outside people say that you're becoming complacent, although you should recognize that no one ever came to work to be complacent that day. There is a loss of "sharpness" in the organization. No one seems to want to tackle the difficult problems they know are there and are reducing effectiveness. They hope the problems will go away, but no one is putting any effort into making them go away. In fact, for the most part, if they are not tackled, they get worse, not better. Things assume a surface significance, but no one delves beneath them. Because everybody is avoiding the difficult, they get on with the easy. So there is lots of happiness, but it's just surface enthusiasm and surface achievement. Nothing significant is being done.

If John had not tackled the three difficult problems he found when he joined the firm, then the organization would still be behaving in a complacent and uncompetitive way. If he hadn't faced up to the issue of the distribution of global brands, then probably that organization would have been forced out of a number of major countries and would have lost a couple of its significant brands.

Links with other Enablers

Although Mystery-Seekers (*see* p. 37) are attracted to problems that have no obvious solution, they tend to be there because of their curiosity for the unknown and situations that no one has met before. Tenacious Challengers head toward a situation because of a drive to get something done. A problem is attractive because it's tough and it represents challenge, but it also represents a stepping stone to some longer-term goal or objective. The contrast here is that the Mystery-Seeker will be interested in something without really knowing where it might lead, whereas the Tenacious Challenger tends to be more focused. It is sometimes the case that Tenacious Challengers score highly in the skill of focusing (*see* p. 115). Like Focusers, they suffer from the risk of getting so locked into their task or objective that they lose sight of the wider world, the wider issues or lose perspective. Like Rottweilers that have seized on to something and can't let go, the Tenacious Challenger may not know when to stop or when to make the strategic withdrawal. To be an effective Tenacious Challenger, therefore, requires you to have a powerful feedback system of people who are unafraid to say, "Time's up!"

Even then it doesn't always work to call a Tenacious Challenger off a problem. A story regarding Dave Packard from the early days of Hewlett-Packard is a good example. While Dave was visiting the HP laboratory that worked on oscilloscope design, he told an energetic young engineer,

Chuck House, that he didn't want to see a particular display monitor on the research bench when he came around to that research facility a year later. What Dave had meant was, "Stop working on this and start working on something more useful." But Chuck, a very Tenacious Challenger, didn't accept this instruction and decided to take a vacation to California. On the way, he stopped off at a number of potential customers for this particular monitor. Their positive reaction to the new monitor convinced Chuck that there was a better way he could honestly respond to Dave's instruction. He decided not to stop work on the device at all, but instead he persuaded his R&D manager to speed the monitor out of the research lab and into production by the time Dave came by again. This meant achieving a then unheard-of turnaround time of nine months compared with what was normally an 18- to 24-month process. The monitor reached sales figures of more than 17,000 units, bringing in $35 million for the company. Several years later at a meeting of HP engineers, Dave presented Chuck with a medal for "extraordinary contempt and defiance beyond the normal call of engineering duty."[15]

How to enhance your ability to tackle tough issues

Motivated by challenge

1. Make a list of the five toughest things you ever did. When you've made that list, work out what was tough about each item for you and also tough for others involved. Is there a pattern in the toughness?

2. Now ask friends and colleagues to do the same. What do you learn about their view of what is tough compared with your view? Has your view of toughness changed over a period of time?

3. Consider how you are at work and how you are away from work. Is tough the same in both places? What is it that attracts you to the challenge? Is it the present tense challenge itself or the future delight of being able to meet the challenge?

Tenacious

1. Think of examples in your own past life where you have really stuck at something. It can be anything that needs repeated and

long-term action or consideration. What made that possible for you? What were the aspects of that particular task or activity that allowed you to keep on working at it? How could you apply this to other areas?

2. Are there problems in your organization (or at least issues) which are recognized by everyone but voiced by no one – the unmentionables? Draw up a list of the unmentionables in your organization. Now speculate: what would happen if the unmentionables got mentioned and then got tackled? What would be the action steps that you could take to tackle some of them?

3. Work with someone where you help them and they help you stick to a particular task or problem. Contract for a minimum period of six months so that both of you can help each other work on whatever the problem or issue is. Before you start, discuss how you are going to cope with times when either of you has a good excuse for not doing something – e.g. illness, overwork, fatigue, boredom, I just don't want to. Find a solution for each of them.

Explore and expand

- If challenges aren't attractive to you, then you can live a very happy life by avoiding them. However, if you want challenges to be more attractive or maybe there are so many challenges you'd better learn to live with some of them, then start with the motivational aspect. How would your attitude need to change for you to find challenges attractive, exciting, etc? Could there be a link to a fear of failure? (*See* pages 32 and 46.)

- Challenges aren't usually solved overnight. Often people don't realize how long they've been working at something, so keep some notes in your calendar. Make a note of the date when you started something and jot down occasionally when you review progress. You may be impressed by how long you do work at things, when perhaps you thought you gave up too soon.

- If you have to do something that you don't want to because it is risky, difficult or tedious, find a way to reward yourself during the process. For instance, when filling in a tax form, eat some chocolates at the completion of each stage – sound more appealing?

Notes

12. BBC Executive Video Seminars, *Transformation*. Quoted by Richard Pascale.

13. Wavell, S. (2000) 'Iceman returns for the long haul,' in *Sunday Times*, January 2, London.

14. *Fortune* (2000). February 7, p. 56.

15. Parkard, D. (1996) *The HP Way: How Bill Hewlett and I Built Our Company*. New York: HarperCollins Publishers, pp. 107–8.

ENABLER 5

CREATE EXCITEMENT

Success is going from failure to failure without a loss of enthusiasm.
Winston Churchill (1874–1965)

Who's having fun?

We once met a man who said he went into HR to get his revenge on people. We thought he was joking – he wasn't! His people didn't like him, they didn't like working for him, they didn't like working in that department at all. The turnover rate in his department was among the highest in the whole company. He behaved as if he hated his job and couldn't wait to get home and soon most of his people learned to do the same. However you looked at it, he brought no excitement into the work. He was definitely not an **Exciter**.

For years we have known two things about people in leadership roles. First, they have to have considerable personal energy. This is because roles of high responsibility are burdensome – they typically involve a lot of travel, a lot of hours, a lot of interactions. Current research and our classroom inquiries suggest that senior managers work 60-hour weeks and typically operate with interactions lasting seven to nine minutes. This is physically draining and requires stamina. (Our colleague David Campbell at the Center for Creative Leadership sees this as well and in fact has incorporated observer ratings of physical energy into his 360-degree survey, the Campbell Leadership Index. His statistics demonstrate that there is a positive relationship between ratings of personal energy and ratings of leadership effectiveness.[16])

So part of the supply for that stamina is having lots of your own personal energy. However, that energy is not simply a physical thing – it's also an attitude. Followers expect leaders to show energy and enthusiasm for the work itself. Exciters inject *enthusiasm* and spontaneity into their work, but alone that is not enough. Just having a high-energy boss doesn't help the rest of the team.

The second area is that the leader effectively *invigorates* the rest of the work team. Let us be clear, that is not about pushing them, although that may happen, too. It is about helping create an environment where other people bring their own energy and excitement to the work. In short, it is about making the work fun and the environment in which that work is done attractive for everyone to bring their own energy and enthusiasm. As Bob Dorn (another colleague at the Center for Creative Leadership) said, "The role of a creative leader is to create an environment where everyone can maximize their own performance." We have known that effective leaders bring their colleagues along emotionally and intellectually. We are simply adding that they should also bring them along energetically.

> People in leadership roles should have considerable, personal energy and effectively invigorate the rest of the work team.

To create excitement you therefore need two skills. Being *enthusiastic* is the part where your bring your own energy and enthusiasm to the role and task of the work. Being *invigorating* is where you create the conditions for others to have fun, enjoy themselves, and bring their own energy to the role – as some would say, to bring joy.

We've noticed that having fun is often seen as an aim for an organization, department, or a leader, but we don't see much evidence of it in reality. In the early 1990s when we first stumbled on to this concept, we used to pose a question to some of our corporate audiences:

> *If you took money out of the equation (that is, you met people's income needs so there was no pressure to move to another organization to get better pay), would your people still come to work for your organization? Would they still come to work for you? Would you still come to work for your own organization?*

We used to get a lot of knowing looks when we asked this question and people used to laugh openly at the question and at us. "These guys are nuts," they would say. To some degree we agreed with our audiences. It was a nutty question in the early '90s. But just look at what has happened since then. In the fastest moving industries, especially those connected to e-business and biotechnology, people get offered share options which are beyond mere salary and day-to-day living expenses. Variable compensation is happening more frequently in other industries, too. Essentially, there are a lot of people in these kinds of organizations who never need to work for a salary again. Yet they continue to work. Why? Well something about the work is more attractive than any other way they could think of to spend their time. These people are truly in the position that we postulated nearly a decade ago, and the thing is, these are quality people who are adding enormous value to their organizations. What we asked then is even more relevant today. Suppose one of your competitors was able to say "yes" to all of our questions. In other words, their people would come in to work because they felt that that organization was the most fun, the most interesting, the best place they could spend their time irrespective of compensation packages. What kind of competitive position would you be in compared to that company?

It seems to us that as the work gets harder, the competition more vigorous, and the pressures tougher, Exciters – people who create the conditions for others to have fun and enjoy themselves – are going to be needed more and more in a wider range of organizations.

Exciters are ...

Exciters create excitement and energy at work not just for themselves but also enthuse others around them.

Signs of Exciters

We have sub-divided Exciters into "enthusiastic" and "invigorating."

Enthusiastic

Tell-tale signs

- Show enthusiasm towards *all* aspects of the job.

- Rarely get "down" or demoralized about things related to their organization or work or the task at hand.

- Show tireless energy to do *all* the work – not just the "big ticket" or important issues.

- Are seen by others as positive and supportive, even when being critical of something that could be done better.

- Seem to enjoy life in the office! Is that weird or what?

Tell-tale actions

- Encourage the enthusiasm of others.

- Bring physical stamina as well as mental and emotional energy to whatever role or task they are tackling.

- Talk about the task or the project or the organization with vigor without being boring.

- Sometimes do something silly that has a positive effect on everyone's morale and energy.

Tell-tale phrases

- "This is exciting."

- "We can do it."

- "I love this business."

- "Isn't it great?"

Invigorating

Tell-tale signs

- People want to work on their teams and project groups.

- Are often associated with laughter – in the office, at meetings, with customers, suppliers, even senior management! They achieve this not because they are good at telling jokes, but because for the most part, people are enjoying working with them.

- Usually people are smiling when they come out of meetings with them.

- See the funny side of Dilbert cartoons, but don't treat people as Dilbert is treated by his boss.

Tell-tale actions

- Find ways to make even the boring bits of work more interesting for themselves or others.

- Won't tolerate tedium – if it is worth doing, it can be interesting.

- Take an interest in how people feel about what they are doing. Without being a "softy," they always look for practical opportunities to improve things for people.

- Often use stories, metaphors or anything else that will communicate a more vivid image.

Tell-tale phrases

- "If it is worth doing, it can be interesting."

- "How can we make this more fun?"

- "What would make this more interesting for you?"

Case study

The case of the impossible project

Bill is the manager of a division of a medium-sized consulting firm. He has approximately 50 people working for him, of which half are consultants and half are administrators. Whenever you see Bill, he is smiling. He bounces into rooms and shows an immediate interest in what others are doing. He listens to difficulties with concern and usually has a helpful suggestion or a new perspective that helps the person to see the difficulty in a new and more positive light. His own work rate is considerable, and if there's a problem, he will be among the last to go home that night if he can help work on the problem or make some kind of positive contribution. Although he travels quite a lot and sometimes works a punishing schedule, whenever co-workers see him, he seems full of energy.

He looks as if he is enjoying himself, and others seem to enjoy working with him on whatever it is he is doing. He is always doing small things that remind people they are human. The other day he came back from Brussels with a large bag of specially made Belgian chocolates. Now, people certainly don't work for chocolate – and he may have ruined a diet or two – but everyone appreciated the gesture. They'd all been working very hard while he was away. When it was the temp's birthday, he insisted that they get a cake and he led the singing. Mary was only there for five days over a two-week period, but she still got treated as one of the family. Earlier this year, they won a new piece of business against a lot of competition, and everyone had put in a lot of work and stayed late to give themselves a chance of getting this work. After getting confirmation of the new business on Tuesday afternoon, people came to work on Wednesday morning to find a bottle of champagne on each of their desks.

The real benefit of what Bill had done for the group emerged when they were offered the opportunity to bid for a huge piece of work – the biggest they'd ever tried for – with an enormous organization that dwarfed them in size. The interesting thing about this particular project was that it was not a crisis. While they had found it was possible to generate amazing amounts of energy and enthusiasm for the short time of a crisis, they all recognized and felt that many of their clients did the same. On this occasion the lack of crisis illustrated the quality of their energy even better.

They needed to demonstrate to this much larger client that they could sustain a heavy workload over a longer duration and could continually come up with creative ideas similar to those which had won them attention in the first place. They were head-to-head with consulting firms much larger, and they knew that their pitch not only had to be good, but they had to demonstrate something about themselves that was unique compared to the other firms. Would their follow-through be good enough?

They offered two additional suggestions to the potential client. First, to work with the client on some existing projects to let them see how the two styles would work together. Second – and this was the clincher – they invited four of the client's people to work with them in their offices to see how they operated on home territory. Total transparency was what they offered. "Join us for everything and anything, see it all." A group of four people came from the client for a series of visits over a three-week period. Everything would be available to the client – nothing hidden or avoided. Bill had said, "Let's have more fun than a Disney ride," and he meant it. But could the client be convinced that their overall approach and way of working would deliver not only the content, but also the quality required?

The consulting firm had asked for only one thing in return – to be told exactly what the visitors said about their experience. They wanted a detailed debrief. The visitors said later that initially they didn't believe what they saw. They thought it was some kind of act to make it seem as if they were all enthusiastic, concerned with making the work and the tasks go well. The consulting firm was invited by the client company to attend the debrief on the basis that they only spoke when invited to.

It was a great day. The visitors were extremely impressed with what they had seen in the consulting offices. They couldn't get over how keen the people were – from the most senior down to the lowliest clerk. They found it hard to believe at first, but soon began to realize that it was genuinely how things operated.

They got the contract, which worked out very well. They were creative, applied and did bring more energy than other consulting firms had brought to the same task. Unexpectedly, they also got another piece of work. They were asked by a senior manager from the client to work with the parent organization on how to become more like them (the consulting firm)! The immediate response was, "You need more people like Bill working for you." It really brought home how much effect Bill had on that department. Before he arrived they were a relatively ordinary group of people doing a reasonably good professional job. Once Bill's influence had spread, they began to realize, by looking in the mirror their clients had held up for them that they really were different – they had an edge. What they were doing was more than just professional competence – there was a level of energy that was just as significant in winning these tough opportunities.

You could try to explain Bill's behavior by saying that he ought to be happy. After all, he has a good job with good staff in a good organization. But I met someone recently who had worked with Bill previously in a different organization that had a lot of troubles and was not a happy place to be. But guess what? Bill was the same there as he is now. It seems to be something that he carries with him whatever the job, role, or circumstances. His approach to managing helps get the best out of people, even when times are tough.

Bill is not the major contributor of new ideas to the group, but he is always keen to sponsor any idea that passes his or others' critical examination. He knows that not all of these ideas will develop into something useful, but he realizes that if he stops supporting ideas, then ideas will not be forthcoming. As a medium-sized organization, they survive because they are more creative and perhaps a little faster than the big competitors in their markets. Therefore, this sponsorship of new ideas, even though some of them don't always work, is a critical part of maintaining energy and commitment to the organization.

What happens when no one creates excitement?

Have you ever worked for someone who disliked their work and who couldn't wait for the time when they could get out of it, retire, move on, or just go home? That's an obvious one. But what about the person who does something not because they want to or see the value in what they are doing, but because they must. They are fulfilling an obligation – which may be real or imagined – to someone else or something else and they don't like it, but they know they have to do it. How much fun is it for you when you must work for someone who must do something? We all know the answer to that one.

The confusing and dangerous irony about working in an environment that has no excitement, no enthusiasm, and is not invigorating is that for a short time an alternative method (e.g. fear and direct pressure) will work. In fact, it will work extremely well, but the costs and consequences of fear or pressure will be felt not just by the individual called to do the work, but also by the organization in which they operate.

If, Bill had treated his job as an ordinary thing with perhaps the odd injection of energy in a crisis, then the consulting firm would never have landed that project or subsequent ones from major customers. The ability to sustain energy in the whole group is not only important for maintaining a level of creativity and application, it's also to do with the quality of people you can attract into that business. A lackluster departmental manager tends to put off the brightest and most enthusiastic staff, while someone like Bill tends to act as a magnet for them.

Links with other Enablers

Energy underlies all that we do. When things are getting tough, we need energy and application to climb the steeper hills. When complex things need explaining, then the qualities of the Simplifier need to be brought into play to bring clarity to fun and enthusiasm (*see* p. 103).

How to create more excitement

Enthusiastic

1. Review what makes you enthusiastic. Sit down and think about it. Create a list of incidents that have made you enthusiastic and brought your energy to the forefront. Now ask other people what they think makes you enthusiastic. Compare the two lists. Do other people see as much enthusiasm as you see in yourself? Or is it the other way around? Explore these two lists extensively to understand how you can develop.

2. Think particularly about your current job and other jobs you have done. What were the parts of those jobs that you found most attractive and easiest to bring energy to? Is there a pattern here? How could you infect the rest of your job with the energy that comes from that one part of it? What would need to shift in the job you do – we're thinking tasks here – to make the job more of an energy-generator?

3. Ask people what they least like about your office, department, or location. Are there things that you could do something about here? Could you compile an action list and get on with it?

Invigorating

1. Think of three people you have enjoyed working for and who have made things invigorating for you. What did they do? Which of those things would work for you?

2. If you are not a spontaneous person, plan to be spontaneous! If appropriate, do something silly one morning. If doughnuts aren't the norm, for example, bring some in. If flowers are not the norm,

put some on each desk. Watch for people's responses and ask for their ideas. If you have a "dress-down day," then how about a "dress-up day?" If you don't dress down, you could suggest it and see how people respond.

3. The next time you have an important meeting with a colleague or two (this works best with just a few people – four is the maximum) don't go to a meeting room or an office, go for a walk. If you work in a tourist area, go on a tourist trip together. If you live near a lake, hire a boat and go on the lake. Whatever it is, have the same serious meeting, but make the conditions different. Now examine what worked and what didn't. How did that change of situation and scenery affect the way the meeting was held?

4. The next time you go to visit someone and their assistant comes to collect you from reception, think of the assistant as an energy reflector. They are reflecting their boss's level of energy. You should be able to gauge how much energy you will be greeted with by carefully observing the level of energy reflected by their assistant. In our coaching work, when we see a client over a period of time, it's easy to forecast the level of energy our client will have on that particular day simply by looking at the energy reflection in their assistant. Energy levels vary on a day-to-day basis. It's useful to be prepared and to know, for instance, whether you are about to be swept off your feet by a high-energy dynamo or to receive a very lackluster reception.

Explore and expand

- Energy is an elusive thing, so watch for it reflected in other people's actions. Get into the habit of measuring the "temperature" of the energy in the room, the department, or the whole business as you walk in.

- Get some trusted people to act as energy monitors for you. We all have low days, so make sure you are aware when they happen, and try to determine why.

- Give yourself some time – put it on your schedule or wait until you are on a long journey – to think about your attitude regarding your work. How much of what you do is really enjoyable? How much would you like to be enjoyable? Is there anything in your job description or contract that says you should not enjoy 100 percent of your work? So how could you convince yourself that seeking out attractive and interesting ways of doing your work could actually lead toward a more effective performance?

Note

16. Campbell, D.P. (1991) *Manual for the Campbell Leadership Index.* Minneapolis, MN: National Computer Systems.

ENABLER 6

BE FLEXIBLE

We are not retreating – we are advancing in another direction.
General Douglas MacArthur (1880–1964)

Flexible Adjusters are not rigid

When Harold Macmillan, the mid-twentieth-century politician and former British prime minister, was asked what made his job difficult but interesting, his reply was just four words: "Events, dear boy, events." He was referring to the demand on politicians and other leaders to respond flexibly to new and unforeseen situations, while still keeping on track with a previously declared policy or strategy. It wasn't the event that would be the undoing of a politician – it would be his or her lack of flexibility in handling that event that would bring them to grief. We call people who have the flexibility to cope with "events," **Flexible Adjusters**.

Mike Harper, when CEO of global food company Conagra, recognized that harvests failed unpredictably. He said that because you could not forecast these events up front, you had to design things – and that included the way the chief executive behaved – so that your company could cope with the shocks and not get badly damaged. Harper insisted that he and his management team must be able to react flexibly to the problems and opportunities their organization faced.[17] This included both things that were not forecast and things that were, but incorrectly.

Ask executive recruiters, human resource generalists, and others whose charge is to identify and select future leaders what they would choose as the one attribute most likely to distinguish high-potential leaders from all the rest. The one attribute that is on almost everyone's list is flexibility.

This is the ability to make adjustments in the face of opposition or mistakes or when apparently otherwise blocked. It is a most important balancing characteristic to any and all other attributes. We found that this skill divided into two parts. The first was being able to *make on-line adjustments*. That is, in mid-project or in mid-process, to recognize that the situation had in some way changed and to make mid-course corrections to cope with it. The other aspect we found was that people who showed a lot of flexibility were also able to *sell change* to their colleagues and therefore create flexibility within the organization.

Probably the most useful of all the eight Enablers, this skill is helpful in any situation. We can't imagine an individual or organization that would be better served without the benefit of this skill. We have been known to call it the "universal compensator." Leaders who demonstrate this category of behavior can balance tenacity/obsessiveness with the realization that they, and others in their organizations, can make mistakes and tackle things differently. One of the major features of those who can be flexible is an ability to sell to others the need to change by reaching out to them, listening, and working with them.

> Flexible Adjusters are probably the most useful of all eight Enablers.

But can you be determined and flexible all at the same time? Of course, but it does require you to incorporate into your managerial style the ability to be open about why you need to be flexible at any particular moment. The reasons why any manager needs to show greater flexibility at some point tend to fall into two categories: events and errors. When some unforeseen event occurs, then the plan clearly needs to be redrafted and rethought. Often there is not much time to do this. In fact, one senior manager described his business environment and the need for change and innovation as ICIC (idea, concept, implementation, correction). According to him, the mission of the organization was to take the best ideas and develop rapid prototypes of goods, products, and services – a concept, as it were. Then, as rapidly as possible, implement the concept and get immediate feedback about any corrections that should be made in the next generation of the product. Another one of our clients echoes this sentiment in his statement to his senior team: "I don't care if you fail, but do it fast!"

So we have entered an era of no time – in actuality, an era of 24/7 (24 hours a day, 7 days a week) – where you and your competitors are likely to see time as inelastic, and where everyone is searching for a way to manufacture time. Lengthy meetings and detailed strategy papers are a luxury.

Sometimes the leader needs to make decisions on the hoof and declare a level of flexibility for the organization. Here's where the selling part becomes crucially important. When there is an error that requires a flexible solution, a deep, sticky pit looms in front of the unwary leader. Admitting the mistake, especially if it's the leader's mistake, is not always easy for people (see pp. 32 and 54). But if you're going to take people with you, they have to know that you understand the situation you are now facing. The only sure-fire way of achieving this is to admit to the things you got wrong and swallow your pride.

Typically, the people who are most confident at being flexible have had the greatest range of experiences. They've started businesses, they've turned around businesses, they've grown businesses. They've been experts, they've been generalists. In ten years of experience, they've had the widest possible variety. Contrast these people with those who have become considerable experts in one area – for instance, they've become great turnaround artists. After ten years they may have had only one year's experience repeated ten times. This puts them in a far less strong position to be able to apply the flexibility that might be needed in one of Harold Macmillan's "events." (*See also* the work on derailment from McCall and Lombardo, 1983.[18])

Flexible Adjusters are ...

Flexible Adjusters are able to make adjustments in the face of problems and to be able to sell those adjustments to others.

Signs of Flexible Adjusters

We have sub-divided Flexible Adjusters into those who make on-line adjustments and those who sell change.

Making on-line adjustments

Tell-tale signs

- Are not rigid in facing problems.
- Do not tend to the "one solution fits all" approach.

- Are prepared to tackle things in a different way, but will only shift for a good reason, and often in discussion with other people. Are not grasshoppers or butterflies in operation, skipping from idea to idea, action to action (i.e. are not "flighty").

Tell-tale actions

- Acknowledge that even in the best of worlds people do make mistakes, and these are not to be denied or hidden, but worked around.

- Shift approaches when necessary.

- Involve other people in helping to find a suitable solution if they feel stuck.

- Acknowledge the importance of other people's ideas.

Tell-tale phrases

- "I got it wrong."

- "Is there another way to look at that?"

- "That's down to me."

- "Let's not get into blame, let's do something about the problem."

- "Let's look at your idea in depth – it's different and it may work."

Selling change

Tell-tale signs

- Show patience and perseverance with people resisting change.

- Take people seriously when they appear to resist change. Want to find real and pragmatic ways to proceed.

- Do not take sides in disputes about who should do what, but seek agreements that benefit the overall project.

- Empathize with all sides in a dispute or argument.

Tell-tale actions

- Acknowledge others' ideas and concerns.

- Take time to explore problem areas with people and to help them understand the need for flexibility and change.

- Work with *all* interested parties to ensure that everyone has bought into the new idea.

- Face up to difficulties that a change may imply and negotiate openly to find a course of action that copes with the difficulties perceived by everyone.

Tell-tale phrases

- "Tell me how this will affect you and how we can achieve the best outcome."

- "How will what you're suggesting benefit that (rival) department?"

- "How can you help bring about the changes?"

- "I understand this change is not easy, so what is a practical way to continue?"

- "Would you rather we did nothing and sank the company?"

Case study

The case of the merging markets

By everybody's estimate it was a long year, but by the end of it, Mary had brought the sales and marketing people of both organizations together in a way that no one else would have believed possible. It was a classic situation. One of the two organizations had separate sales and marketing departments. The other legacy company had merged these two functions years ago. One organization put considerable emphasis on geographic regions, whereas the other was business-segment-focused, so treated geographic regions fairly lightly and saw no problem with one region dealing with another region's customers if it made life better for the customer. All of the sales and marketing departments were merged into one grand customer development department, but still contained all of the directors from the previous structures. All of the directors talked integration but walked independence.

Mary had been put in charge of the whole thing, having come from one of the companies. She knew both organizations quite well and the previous year had convinced her, before she even knew about her present job, that the new merged organization had to get much more serious about integration. So far it had lived under the pretense of a merged department which struggled to carry on as it did before. A more radical integration solution was necessary, given the way the markets and a certain customer were shifting.

The great thing about the way Mary operated during the year was that although she encouraged a lot of tough talking, and she did a lot herself, she never let things get to the point of explosion, although the fuses felt mighty short on several occasions! Issues usually emerged about how flexible each person or each group could be. No one likes giving up what they had worked for and understood. From Mary's point of view, it must have seemed like a lot of resistance.

She talked one-to-one with most of the staff concerned in each department. She listened carefully and took people's concerns seriously. In a few cases that took a lot of patience, which had probably not been shown to those individuals before. Her approach, though brusque, had a positive motivational effect. People started to believe in the new organization.

Mary didn't get everything right. However, when she did get something wrong (e.g. she made a suggestion that wouldn't work or she didn't take some aspect into account when making a decision), she always admitted her mistake and was open about what had to be done next. Her openness made it easier for several of her colleagues to suggest that maybe they hadn't quite got everything right themselves in the past. The working atmosphere, although pressured, became less tense and they started to get breakthroughs.

They thought they were well on track by the third quarter, when their biggest customer dropped a bombshell. They wanted an integrated sales and marketing support facility and they wanted to deal with one person. Previously, three or four separate members of different sales and marketing teams had been toiling along to the door. The customer complained that they spent their time telling sales staff the latest news that surely they ought to be aware of: "This can't go on," they said. "We want to deal with a single source and a single person to head up that source."

It has to be said that this was the long-term aim for the reorganization, but they were nowhere near achieving it yet. Late night meetings followed and there was talk of a quick-fix solution by creating a special post to deal specifically with this one customer. However, Mary kept very cool and helped people realize that this was the incentive they needed to make the reorganization really work. They could prove to those people who had doubted so far that this was definitely the way the world was moving. This is what all customers were going to expect in the future. If they panicked and created a one-off solution, they would be patching up solutions for as far as they could see into the future. But this was a tough and unprecedented situation they were facing now.

It was over the next two months that Mary really demonstrated why she had been chosen for the job. She worked with the customer and with the heads of sections who now reported to her. She looked for flexible solutions to the myriad of problems that existed – computer systems were incompatible, reporting systems didn't match, order systems and delivery systems were not easily reconcilable between the two companies. Mary also spent a huge amount of time internally selling the changes that were needed and invigorating the people who needed to make those changes. There were some very tough conversations and some people got quite disgruntled, but in the end they recognized the force of the argument that she, aided by their customer's demand, were putting forward. Change came about in small and large jumps. By the end of the year they were in a position not only to meet the customer's need, but also to offer the same service to many other customers.

Could the company have done this without Mary? Yes, probably, although not in anything like the timescale that was actually achieved. Did they make mistakes on the way? Yes, of course, but the speed of movement and their ability to admit mistakes and respond to them meant that they always achieved more. For every three steps forward, they went one step back, but they learned something useful from each of those backward steps. They didn't make the same mistake twice.

I'd heard Mary described as a good person to have around when the going got tough. I hadn't realized quite what was meant by that. She certainly showed that individuals and the company as a whole could be a lot more flexible when the need arose than anyone had previously realized.

What happens when no one is flexible?

"It's a little like mountain climbing," said a source close to the board. "Anyone can get to a certain level, but very few can function well in the really rare air." "He took pride in managing for the long haul – but that made him unyielding in the face of immediate circumstances and while he was in command of a vast number of details, he seemed to lose sight of the big picture." "He was blind to his own weaknesses and unwilling to take advice. He became increasingly isolated and obsessed with controlling the tiniest details."

The quotes above are from an article in *Fortune* (January 2000) about Doug Ivester, who left Coca-Cola in December 1999, having spent only two years as its chief executive. The basic point of the article is that although Ivester was a brilliant man and as chief financial officer had in the previous ten years dazzled Chief Executive Officer Roberto Goizueta with his hard work and creative execution of company strategy, once he got to the top job, he showed a lack of flexibility necessary to cope with an organization of this size facing a number of critical issues.

It would be interesting to speculate whether there are different kinds of flexibility at different levels. Perhaps Ivester showed the right levels of flexibility on his way up through the finance department. But when he made it to the chief executive's role, perhaps his flexibility was not sufficient for what was needed.

A senior manager lacking flexibility can block a lot of other good work going on in the organization by more junior managers. Sometimes that lack of flexibility owes its origin to a long period of success. We are all vulnerable to the assumption that because we have got it right for five, six, ten, or however many years, then we will know how to get it right always. It is easy to believe we have found the formula, and all that life involves is applying it in larger and larger situations. Our research overwhelmingly suggests that you adopt that strategy at your own peril.

Links with other Enablers

If you're going to try to bring about change and flexibility, it almost certainly helps to be clear with everyone exactly what changes are needed. People leading major change will value the skills of the Simplifier either for themselves or as part of their team (*see* p. 103). Equally, the ability to scan ahead (*see* p. 62) and spot potential problems together with being risk tolerant are useful attributes when unforecastable change is necessary (*see* p. 52). There is a danger, however, that the very risk-tolerant manager heads off into situations that their staff find overly risky or overly frightening. The Flexible Adjuster will make only the changes that are really necessary – those that are reasonable, intelligent risks – and will be able to sell those changes so that other people take them up and make them work. Being flexible does not imply pushing change into place in the face of opposition.

How to be more flexible

Making on-line adjustments

1. Choose a relatively low-impact decision – one that has not much risk attached to it. Work with a colleague to find a different way of tackling that decision. Implement the decision in a different way and see how it feels.

2. Look for opportunities to make immediate adjustments to your operating style, in both content and process. For instance, halfway through a meeting you are chairing (but not at the trickiest spot), stop the proceedings and ask, "How could we make the second half of this meeting better than the first half?" Encourage everyone to speak, not just the loudest and the most extroverted around the table. There is probably a useful contribution from everyone, and if there isn't, why are they there anyway?

3. Ask someone who knows you well to what extent they see you being able to change in mid-path. Ask them to give examples of where they have seen you changing and if they can, examples where they think you should have changed but didn't. Compare it with the list you have made for yourself before the discussion.

Selling change

1. In the middle of some kind of discussion or dispute or negotiation, put yourself in the other person's shoes. How do they view you across the table/room? How do they view your line of argument? How do they view your colleagues and the substance of the argument you have put forward? Now review your own approach from their point of view. Would you make any changes?

2. Let someone sell you something that you had previously decided against. Make it something trivial so that it doesn't matter if you

see this as "losing," but understand the feeling of having an idea sold to you where you had already made a decision. How does it feel? Can you empathize with how other people feel when you are trying to sell them an idea when they have already made up their minds?

3. Having laid out your own point of view, take some time out to play devil's advocate. (Choose your subject and your moment with care – you don't want people to think you are certifiably opposed to everything!) Explore what it's like to create arguments against yourself and see how viable they could be. What could you learn about greater flexibility in the way you oppose an idea? (Try this out with a teenager you know.)

Explore and expand

- Flexibility is often in the eye of the beholder. Keep notes on your approach to a particular problem before, during, and after. When you look back on it with the benefit of hindsight, how flexible were you on the spot? What other approaches might you have taken?

- How much time do you give to helping other people make changes? This is especially important to know if you are flexible yourself, especially if you have difficulty understanding why it takes other people so long to come around to what is for you an obvious decision.

- Review again how easily you can admit to mistakes. Do you give yourself permission to admit your mistakes? Who are you prepared to admit them to? Can you admit you were wrong to your bosses or your followers more easily? Do you have a hierarchy that determines who you'll admit things to?

Notes

17. Tyler, N. (1991) *Leadership Video: John Kotter.*

18. McCall, M. and Lombardo, M. (1983) "What makes a top executive?" in *Psychology Today*, 17(2), 26–31.

ENABLER 7

BE A SIMPLIFIER

I adore simple pleasures. They are the last refuge of the complex.

Oscar Wilde (1893) A *Woman of No Importance*

Making the complex simple

"I still remember when old George said ..." Unless you avoid all social functions, you cannot fail to have heard some version of this phrase when people get together and look over their shared histories. People remember phrases and one-liners easily and apparently forever. We'll bet you can still sing a silly advertising jingle from a campaign that's more than a decade old, even though it has had precisely zero minutes of air time in the last ten years. Go ahead, try it right now – jot down a few examples.

We remembered these lines from advertisements shown in the US:

- "Just do it." (Nike)
- "Two all-beef patties, special sauce, lettuce, cheese, pickles, onions, on a sesame seed bun." (McDonald's)
- "Can you hear me now?" (Verizon)
- "Think different." (Apple)

Because they are short and simple, we remember them easily.

We are not talking about the simplistic. We're referring to the kind of simple that a child demands when it asks you for an explanation of the world. Children frequently ask "why?" and often there is no good, deep, simple answer to give. "It depends" or "Because I say so" are really not satisfactory responses. Really profound simplicity has a powerful effect on everyone who hears it. We have talked in the past about resonant simplicity and you only have to watch or hear a great speaker to appreciate how the right words chosen in a simple but deep manner can convey a long-lasting and very energizing image. The great politicians and preachers have the ability to make their words convey a meaning that is at the same time easy to grasp and which resonate with the listeners' innermost feelings, expectations, and beliefs. It is our belief that no matter how pretty computer-aided displays get, there is far less resonant simplicity in an "all singing and dancing" presentation than there is in some well-chosen words.

> It's essential in the fast-moving organization for people to get the message immediately ...

As the speed with which organizations operate continues to increase and the quantity of communication increases in parallel, any message you wish to send your colleagues or your customers is now competing with many more messages than it has before. In early 2000 in the US, it was estimated that the number of advertising minutes on television had jumped one minute in a year to almost 17 minutes per prime-time hour! With commercials being as short as 15 seconds, that's as many as 68 advertisements per hour. So if you are able to offer a message that is simple but easy to understand and makes sense to the reader or listener immediately, you are at a competitive advantage in the communications race. Fast-moving organizations can't afford their people to spend part of their time checking to see if they have understood something correctly, going back for clarification, and generally not being sure of what they heard the first time. It's essential in the fast-moving organization for people to get the message immediately and be able to act on it with no second thoughts or doubts. So communicating accurately but simply is a key skill in any organization today. Albert Einstein, although working in a field of almost unimaginable complexity, put simplicity very high on his list of priorities. His three rules of work were:

1. Out of clutter find simplicity.

2. From discord find harmony.

3. In the middle of difficulty find opportunity.[19]

Our research suggests that the way **Simplifiers** are able to convey ideas and information simply yet completely results from capability in three sub-skills. It starts with the ability to understand the fundamentals of something - *essence detectors* get to the core of the description. They fundamentally understand the system, the politics, the psychology – in short, the essence of whatever it is that is being described. Unfortunately, people who are only good at essence detection may not be able to explain what they understand deeply and fundamentally to anybody else. To be useful to others, the essence detector skill needs to be combined with the skill of making things clear and not getting the message too complex or in the wrong order. *Clarifiers* ruthlessly eliminate any ambiguity and uncertainty in written or spoken communication. However, if they just did that, anything they produced would look like a legal document. Even though ambiguities will have been painfully ironed out, it's not usually an easy read. The clarity has to be brief and clear as well as simple and clear. Generally, therefore, to make the whole thing palatable to another person who knows nothing about the subject, the third skill of translating complex topics into vivid symbols or metaphors so that everyone can understand them is needed. *Interpreters* use symbols, metaphors, or images that communicate ideas crisply and easily. By working through the previous skills, they are able to convey a complex message by analogy or with a short story so that other people can grasp the essential message and information that is being communicated. Interpreters are always aware of their audience and manage the style of their communication to suit the needs of their audience.

Our first test of an effective Simplifier is simple. Could you communicate your message to a sensible seven-year-old child? If you could not, then probably your employees will be missing out on some of the data, too. Our second test asks, "Does the communication resonate?" If you pluck a piece of catgut approximately 40cm long, it makes a small noise. If you wrap up the noise that catgut makes in a wooden box made by Stradivarius, then the sound will resonate throughout the largest concert halls. Resonance is about catching some kind of built-in frequency or built-in empathy for the message and making it echo that message around the organization. You can see resonance in action every time there's scandal or gossip flying round. It was a very small piece of data usually at the start, but doesn't it just increase so easily?

In today's organizations it becomes important to bridge short attention spans and be able to communicate the essence of an idea in a few words or ringing phrases. In the last 20 years, the average sound bite has gone from over one minute to (with the advent of Twitter) 280 characters. It's also important for a manager (and anyone else who wants to influence people) to be able to win both the minds and the hearts of everyone in the organization. This is impossible if the leader can only communicate with people at the top or people who know all about the subject anyway.

Simplifiers are found in every leadership situation. Some of the clearest examples we have seen are in the teaching and communications professions. Our colleague Bill Drath at the Center for Creative Leadership is a good example. When a scientist has an article they wish to write, they go and talk to Bill. He encourages them to summarize the entire paper on to a single page – that's correct, several thousand words on a single sheet! It's tough – it doesn't make sense when you first talk to Bill, but if you can convey the whole of your article or even your book in a single page, you're certain you have got to the essence of it and you'll certainly have a good chance of communicating it. The publisher Pearson Education has a rule that their salespeople should be able to summarize the meaning and value of each book they sell in 25 words or less. They have started taxing their authors with the same challenge: Can you put what might be five years of research and a book of 70,000 words into a 25-word sentence? By the way, Pearson also has a rule that says the sentence must not start with "an important contribution to ..." Pick up your annual report or a significant piece of writing about your organization and its purpose, mission, vision, strategy. Can you summarize that in 25 words or less? Has your organization's writer tried to do the same? We will come back to this area when we discuss how to enhance the skills of simplifying (*see* p. 112).

Before we leave this area, let us not forget the many fine examples of simple, clear communication offered in advertising campaigns and political speeches. As we illustrated at the beginning of this section, we can all remember a favorite advertising slogan and probably one or two phrases that politicians knowingly spoke into the airwaves. Once upon a time, it was the case that a politician made the speech and the news media selected out a sound bite from within that speech. Now, of course, we have all realized the importance of sound bites and their relevance to the shorter news bulletins we hear. In fact, CNN, having made their mark with "All News, All the Time," has led us to believe that politicians and other public figures manufacture their speeches (and their personalities!) around sound bites. Nonetheless, the intention is equally the same as putting your strategy into 25 words or explaining to a child why they can't have all the toys they want.

Simplifiers are ...

Simplifiers are able to get to the essence of something and to communicate it to others in such a way that they not only understand it, but become enthused and committed to it.

Signs of Simplifiers

We have sub-divided Simplifiers into "essence detectors," "clarifiers," and "interpreters."

Essence detectors

Tell-tale signs

- Always get to the core of an issue.
- Look for the profound rather than the impressive – the simple underlying the simplistic.
- Know that, paraphrasing Einstein, the level of thinking at which you understand a problem is deeper than the level at which you first discover it.
- Want to know what the true essentials are in any situation or with any problem.

Tell-tale actions

- Cut through the complexity to understand the fundamental components.
- Look for straightforward ways to communicate a message.
- Capture ideas and strategies in an *image* or a *slogan*.
- Identify patterns in complex or confusing situations that help the process be understood.
- Use the least jargon and fully explain any jargon used.

Tell-tale phrases

- "So the fundamental issue is ..."
- "The core of the problem is ..."
- "What are the essentials?"

Clarifiers

Tell-tale signs

- Strive to be clear and precise without being wordy.
- Seem to understand their audience and how they will read/hear a message.

Tell-tale actions

- Speak concisely and briefly without being superficial.
- Take trouble to find the best ways to say things.
- Often rewrite what they have written and usually are the toughest critics of their own work.

Tell-tale phrases

- "How can we say that in fewer words?"
- "I'm not clear about this yet."

Interpreters

Tell-tale signs

- Find it easy to explain complex subjects simply enough for children to understand.
- Try to engage the audience's imagination and allow their imaginations to shape the explanation.
- Are not afraid of the vivid or on occasion the dramatic.

Tell-tale actions

- Use metaphors and images – actually, anything that helps to translate a message to someone else.

- Listen for resonance from the audience to confirm that they have understood.

Tell-tale phrases

- "Let me put it another way."

- "If you compare it to ..."

- "I want you to prioritize ..."

Case study

The case of the bothered builder's depot

The company supplying materials to the building trade had been successful for many years, but now was in a state of total confusion. The long-serving previous CEO had called in three different sets of consultants, randomly hired new blood, changed strategy about every six months, and when he was finally pushed into a retirement condominium within earshot of a warmish part of an ocean, the rest of the company hadn't the faintest idea of where they were going or why.

Dave, the new CEO, impressed everyone in his first week by the simple, straightforward way he answered questions about himself and his aims for the ailing business. He told them, "I won't have much to say until I have really found out what our situation is and worked out how we can and should move forward."

There followed a period of several months when Dave seemed to turn up just about everywhere. He was in the head office, at depots, riding in delivery trucks, talking to customers, talking to suppliers, visiting sites around the country large and small. He talked with everyone and asked thousands of questions. He wanted examples, stories, and diagrams. He was always asking how and why. (Talk about enthusiasm! But that's a different story and a different Enabler.) Then in a few words or using a diagram, he'd summarize what he'd heard. "Is it like that?" he'd continually ask. Pretty soon he had the reputation as a first-class listener who seemed to grasp the whole picture right down to the detail really quickly. This in turn encouraged people to tell him things that perhaps they hadn't mentioned to previous top managers. Dave really did get an insight into the whole story.

Over what later came to be called the "renewal week," Dave held meetings with representatives of all the divisions of the firm. He continued to question and listen, but now he was trying out some of his thoughts: "If we did this, how would that affect our margin?" or "If we canceled that, how would it affect our customers?" Finally at the end of that week, he emerged from a short board meeting and called everyone in the office together. His first statement was a classic piece of simplicity in action:

"As you know, I have traveled around this whole organization over the last few months trying to understand it and to discover what it is we really have here. I have discovered that many of you are confused and uncertain as to how we should move forward or indeed what our plans are. So let me try and put some of that straight. I think this company is like an attic of a large old house. We've got a lot of stuff up there, mainly covered in dust, and we don't know what is there and what isn't. We've probably got an enormous amount of valuable stuff up there, but until we can actually see our way around the attic, until we dust off the things, we won't know. So I propose an action plan which is very simple. We will illuminate and we will appreciate. We will illuminate the attic by installing all kinds of ways of measuring what we have and creating a greater transparency of information in the company. We will then appreciate what we really have and value it properly and understand how we can make best use of not only the things and inventory we have, but also the many skills and attitudes that exist among our workforce who do wonderful work that we probably don't appreciate properly.

We therefore will go through three stages. First, we will clear out from the attic the things that we don't need, the things that are useless, the things that are too old to be useful. I will set several working groups in action to establish how to achieve this. Second, we will clean up the attic, make it tidy, understand where our major customers are, understand our major sources of revenue, understand our cash flows, understand the finances generally. Third, we will build up the attic. There are many areas in which we are under-utilizing our skills. We need to develop and grow new clients, new markets, and new customer opportunities.

Over the next few months, I am setting up project groups and working parties to develop our ideas and put into practice all three areas. I expect all of you to give your best in helping us open up our business to make it the envy of all our competitors. Oh, and by the way, I've drawn a picture or two to summarize this ..."

What happens if no one acts as a Simplifier?

People are confused. They don't know what the strategy is, they don't understand what goals the company is seeking – they rely on rumors. People in the organization don't coordinate with each other because they don't have common motives or objectives. Companies post-merger (where both previous organizations had clear goals and clear approaches) can often go through this stage. They want to know what the new merged company is aiming for and what the strategy for the future will be. People don't know what the new organization should really be like or how it will really turn out. People make judgments about their leader's communication style, and it is here that the three sub-skills of Simplifier are often significantly missing.

When *essence* skills are missing in the leader, people don't feel that person is on top of the problem. They don't feel grounded. They are doubtful if the leader really has a full grasp of the situation, and if they are not clear on the situation then no one else trusts the leader's recommendation for the solution to it.

When *clarifier* skills are missing in the leader, different groups disagree on their diagnosis of the situation and what to do about it. Goals tend to be specific to parts of the organization and unknown in other parts. No overall sense of strategy exists, and the best that most people can do is to muddle through on a day-to-day basis.

When *interpreter* skills are missing, people think of their organization as grey, purposeless, perhaps even rudderless. There are no symbols, metaphors, or any kind of vivid image evolved by the organization. At social events, people are almost embarrassed to admit who they work for.

If Dave had not been clear, simple, and reasonably vivid in what he wanted to do, his speech would have seemed like any of those produced by the three groups of consultants who the previous chief executive had hired. Dave understood that a major report was not needed at that moment, but some clarity and motivation was. Immediately after his speech every part of the organization resonated with his ideas, and everyone was able to contribute. Without that skill the organization would have limped through another consulting report and probably soon would have faded from sight.

Links with other Enablers

Simplifier skills, because they are about communication, can be applied in conjunction with the other Enablers. For instance, when flexibility is needed in the organization, selling change may involve being clearer than you were before about what is really being faced and what the options are. Alternatively, the effective futurist may well want to communicate what they have seen in a clearer and more vivid way than they first understood it (*see* Enabler 3, p. 62). Of course, it is often very invigorating to understand more clearly than you did before exactly what the company's strategy is, what its sales successes have been, how everyone can bring in their efforts to contribute to the overall organizational goals.

How to be a better Simplifier

Essence detectors

1. Take a communication that you or someone else has produced about company policy or strategy and rewrite it as a telegram in less than 25 words. When you review this (we're sure you're used to reviewing by now), ask yourself, "How easy or how hard is this?" Did the difficulties, if any, have to do with you not fully understanding the strategy, or was it about condensing it into a few words?

2. When you are chairing a meeting, at the end of each item ask the group to produce a ten-word slogan to summarize the action or other outcomes of that item. Discuss with your colleagues any difficulties and why those difficulties arise.

3. The next time you are asked to make a company presentation, instead of wheeling out the computer-generated graphics, do it as a simple speech with as few illustrations as you can manage. Promise yourself to use no bullet points, but use as many diagrams and pictures as you can. How did that feel? Ask your audience how well you communicated the message.

Clarifiers

1. Imagine that you are a contributor to the *Encyclopedia Galactica* in the year 2100 and you have only one sentence to describe the whole history of your company. What would you write? Share the exercise with a couple of colleagues. What did they write? What did you learn?

2. The next time you have to give a presentation, do it as a story. You can use a story in a chronological order from beginning through middle to end, but you can also tell the story as an adventure, a detective novel, or a piece of history looking back from a future date.

3. Go to your favorite news sources and capture some headlines from articles where the headline clearly and simply describes what follows in the article. Put the headlines away in a separate place from the articles. About a week later read the articles again and invent your own headlines. Now compare your headline to the one that was written by the editor. How effective were you? Now have someone read your headline and the original – wait for honest feedback.

Interpreters

1. Before writing your next report, interview at least one person who will receive your report and get them to tell you the key questions they want answered in that report. Write at least part of the report as question and answer – a kind of dialog – rather than in the normal format.

2. When you have to explain something to someone, look for more vivid images that will help in the explanation. Think how this item would appear from the perspective of a customer, a person from another culture, or a small child. Keep looking for different perspectives on the same item until you find one that's vivid enough to convey your meaning.

3. Suppose you could use only pictures without words. How would you describe something in cartoon picture images? How could you make the action in the cartoon tell the story?

Explore and expand

- Assess how important it is for you to convey ideas clearly, simply, and cleanly. To what extent does your job require you to communicate significant ideas to other people? Chart back over the last three months and think of significant occasions when by conveying a message clearly and simply you will have saved people time, avoided a problem, or gained an advantage over a competitor. Work out for yourself how strategically important this skill is to your particular role at the moment.

- Now do the same thing, but test other people's points of view about how important it is for them that you can convey ideas clearly and simply. Ask a valued colleague to give you some examples of where you have conveyed your ideas clearly and simply. Also (if you are up to it) ask for examples where you haven't, but should have done. See if you can develop a sense of the situation that needs the extra effort to make things clear and simple. Understanding when it is worth putting in the effort and when it is not would be a key advantage, especially if simplifying does not come – well, simply.

- From time to time, deliberately set aside something you have written or make a recording of what you have said and store it for at least six months. Then review it. Over a period of a year at least, you will get a sense of whether you are improving or not by reviewing these "blasts from the past." You can be as critical of yourself as anyone. Take a look at how you were communicating then and whether it comes up to your present standards. (By the way, this can also be a wonderful way to review your improvement in becoming a Future-Scanner.)

Note

19.   Russel, R. *Dow Theory Letters*. LaJolla, CA.

ENABLER 8

BE FOCUSED

*Obstacles are those frightful things you see when you take
your eyes off your goal.*

Henry Ford (1863–1947)

What won't we do today?

Death by a thousand initiatives. Too much to do with too few resources in too little time. Or as the Dutch say, "too much hay on the fork." This is the condition of many people in organizations today. But what of the leader's role in this dilemma? A person who is comfortable with focus or who possesses the ability to focus is able to keep an eye on a few specific objectives, no matter what else may be going on. In the extreme, **Focusers** may be accused of being obsessive about time or about certain tasks. Doing only what is seen as important at a given point in time is what they are best at. We often have double standards when it comes to the value of Focusers in organizations. Being blind to all but the most important objectives can be a nuisance at the time. It can mean that your idea or project gets pushed down the priority list. Focusers are usually celebrated in the long run after the project or piece of work is completed, but are easily criticized at the moment when the project goes awry because of unforeseen circumstances. A lack of breadth of vision can often be the perceived consequence, and in truth it is not easy to say at the time, especially when under pressure, where focus ends and obsession begins.

Sometimes it is difficult to tell at the early stages in organizations what is a focused and appropriate use of priorities and what is obsession. Was Trevor Baylis, the British inventor, ex-stunt man, circus performer, international swimming competitor, and entrepreneur, obsessive in spending 12 years perfecting the clockwork radio? While watching a BBC *Panorama* program about AIDS in Africa, he realized the enormous potential that bringing radio communication to communities where no reliable electrical supply existed would have. His work made a major improvement to communication, education, and healthcare awareness in many developing countries. Yet Baylis's ideas were turned down by Philips International, BP, Marconi, and the Design Council among others. But despite these and other refusals and turndowns, Baylis kept on developing the radio and finally won financial support for the project.[20]

> In the extreme, Focusers may be accused of being obsessive about time or certain tasks.

As Markos Tambakeras, Chief Executive of Kennametal Inc. in Latrobe, Pennsylvania, describes it to stock analysts and employees, "We can't afford to do ten things OK. We must do three or four things exceptionally well." Involved in a turnaround situation, Markos is looking for any edge to grow his business in a marketplace where there are only a few international competitors, where margins are slim, and where today's technological advantage is tomorrow's commodity – everybody expects your product to contain that feature. It's hard to see how many organizations can be in anything but turnaround or start-up mode in today's organizational world. There is hardly any stability now – you are either trying to invent, improve or tear things apart and start all over. Focused behaviors and actions are what keep the organization on target, working and moving toward some deliverable product or service. (They are the driving forces that keep the conflicting pieces of the organization moving together.)

Executives at Corning Glass use a slogan they call "the critical few." It is their current list of the four or five issues, tasks, or strategic initiatives that everyone in the organization must be aware of and must pay attention to. The items on the list are critical because everybody understands that each issue or action is important to the organization's future. The significance of there being few items on the list is that it is feasible for everyone to incorporate a few things into their action plans and priorities, whereas a long list of activities would never get incorporated. Does "the critical few" change? Yes, of course. Tasks get completed and new issues emerge. But Corning has the focus, determination, and courage not simply to add items to the "few," but to drop things off as well. The "few" stays few in number, which is the only way that everyone can hope to include these items into their own personal agendas. (Of course, this connects well with Simplifying *see* p. 103).

As many leaders will tell, if you want to keep things focused, then you have to be able to deal with conflict. The conflict arises easily enough. Different people each have different urgencies, which translate into different priorities. Imagine the scene: your two brightest direct reports are pointing in opposite directions about how your departmental meeting should spend its time. Each wants the larger piece of the "time pie." As their manager you have to find some kind of resolution to the dispute. So what are your priorities for the departmental meeting? Which of these two ideas is more important? Or is there a third one more important still? In our experience, few of us relishes conflict, but some step up to it easier than others. Leadership, however, requires that decisions will have to be made about the organization's choices/direction, and that will engender conflict. Of course, choosing not to make choices is a choice, too, but that's a different story.

Focusers are ...

Focusers know what are the few most important things to do or keep a watchful eye on no matter what else may be going on and however many options beckon.

Signs of Focusers

Tell-tale signs

- Understand at any time which are the "critical few" things that need to be done.

- Will shift focus when necessary and will abandon the previous "critical few" when they are no longer critical.

- Are not overly detail-driven, but can accommodate detail when it becomes critical.

- Learn the right level at which to apply their focus; i.e. a CEO might focus on relations between divisions, while a divisional VP might focus on specific operations.

- Understand that focusing, when overdone, can be perceived as obsession.

- Are good at knowing what not to do.

Tell-tale actions

- Stick to the point; know where the goal is.

- Choose what they want to focus on, even when it may not be what everyone else wants to focus on.

- Instinctively recognize the high leverage points in any system.

- Think of using their time as a process of investment; i.e. invest time rather than spend it and certainly don't waste it.

- Do a few things really well and are not distracted by trivia.

Tell-tale phrases

- "So the point is ...?"

- "How can we invest our time better?"

- "I don't think that's important."

Case study

The case of the overseas obsessive

With our luggage still around us – there had been a delay checking into the hotel so we brought everything here to the office – we made our first review of the business. "Where do we start?" we asked ourselves glumly.

Our consulting firm had agreed to help turn around a shoe manufacturing business in a country, culture, and time zone far, far away from where we normally operated. "It'll be a developmental opportunity for you," my senior partner had whispered in my ear. Oh, the perfidious phrase!

For the next few weeks, the whole thing seemed, to my inexperienced eye, a terrible mess. We had to work through translators to talk to many of the staff – it was tedious and slow. It could result in a morning that produced absolutely no useful information at all. But time and again Alex seemed to know who to talk to, what to ask, and when to go back to ask again if something wasn't clear. Her behavior was in marked contrast to the way our team leader operated. We called him "last chance Larry" because it was widely rumored that he'd been given this project as a stay of execution. If this baby didn't fly, then Larry would – straight out of the ninth floor window! Larry was a true obsessive. First in, hardly ever out, he seemed to live the whole of his life in the building that became our temporary base for the three months we were there. He was into everything and it was that which contrasted him so obviously with Alex. She would work long hours with the rest of us, but as the days went by, it became very clear that she really was making progress with her focused approach.

Whereas Larry, despite his long hours, didn't really seem to have a clue about what he or we should put our energy into. He kept issuing bulletins and briefings and deadlines, each saying something different from the previous offering: "We should concentrate on the finance;" "the problem was in the marketing department;" "the basic strategy needed revising;" "there was corruption among the suppliers;" "the manufacturing competencies were inadequate." On and on Larry went, roaming freely through every possible corner of the management skills archive. Soon we got to the point that every time Larry called us together for another briefing or pep talk we'd mentally roll our eyes and prepare to throw out the work we'd just been devoted to – "this afternoon's unswerving priority," as one wag put it – and wait to be briefed on what tomorrow's unswerving priority was going to be.

Then came the breakthrough. After about a month, we could see where and why the costs were escalating and the sales diminishing. What to do? Larry, of course, wanted to implement a 23-point plan. He was our boss, and 23 points was an awful lot of action, and action counted well in our Manhattan head office. Also all these actions would take a lot of time. From our point of view that was what we were paid for, so definitely no problems there – although some of us did wonder if this business could really afford our costly attention for much longer.

Larry walked us through the 23-point action plan at a major meeting that lasted most of the day. It took a long time because many of us had reservations to resolve before we could agree to it. So it was fascinating when later that evening in the bar, Alex offered us a quite different version of what we should do ...

"Just four things to focus on," she said. It would be quick and while not pain free, it would liberate the company to run on its own within the next two weeks. There would be problems and the company would falter, but if all of the remaining employees could focus on just these four areas, then not only could they pull through, but they should actually begin to grow.

It was interesting to watch the reaction in our group. Larry, of course, was against it – 23 actions was what was needed and what his future depended on. However, at least half of us would rather have adopted Alex's plan. Essentially, her idea was to spend a lot of time helping key players in the business to understand how they could explain her four focus areas to everyone in the organization, then to develop ways of charting progress, and finally to face up to some of the inevitable problems that would occur along the way. Her mixture of tough honesty and simple pragmatism seemed to be what this organization needed. Many of us felt that her plan, while much simpler and generating less revenue for our consulting business, would actually have given the shoe company a real change and a real chance of survival.

Alex was overruled, of course. Why turn down fee-earning days that are staring you in the face? She left the company within 18 months and I lost touch with her. The last I heard, she'd gone into e-business start-ups. I gather she's on her third one now, 50 million dollars richer and still asking people to focus on just a few points!

The shoe company gamely tried to apply the 23-point plan, paid us a lot of money and was in receivership within nine months of our leaving. If Alex had had her way, I wonder what would have happened ...

Focus for survival or more

It seems that being focused is not just a business survival issue – it may be a life survival issue. There is some evidence that in sea and air disasters, passengers have survived because they have stayed completely focused on the business of following the lights to the exit, following the corridor to the door, or following the way to the stairway. This focus was so strong that it allowed them to ignore the fact that the boat or the airplane had become inverted (i.e. down was up and up was down) and possibly in some cases meant swimming underwater to reach the next exit. The evidence suggests that those few people who have survived such disasters were able to do so, not because they were in better physical shape or because they were stronger or otherwise more robust, but simply because they were more focused.

What happens when no one focuses?

People who teach strategy know that saying "no" is often a more powerful choice when it serves to keep the organization focused on what it does (or can do) best. One of our colleagues at New York University, Tom Mullen, used to say, "The essence of strategy is denial." So a great strategy tells you at least as much about what *not* to do as *what* to do. When focus is not

... being focused is one of the keys to making a fast-moving organization work.

available, rain-dance rules emerge. What are rain-dance rules? It's where an organization that is not focused substitutes something else. Someone notices that a particular action – say, allowing salespeople to wear casual dress – appears to link to a particular outcome – e.g. an increase in sales. So a rule gets created. Mostly no one knows why the rule is created and often they can be created by hunch rather than by clear evidence. For example, the coincidence of some action – let's say, dancing – preceding a desired result, e.g. rain. So people believe that the dancing caused the rain. In organizations it's easy for certain actions to coincidentally precede some desired outcome and then get turned into rules. The problem is that the rules now take the place of what should be the goal, and everybody focuses on keeping to the rules rather than on achieving the goal. To be effectively focused there is no substitute for the clarity of a long-term goal or mission. If you don't know what you're trying to achieve in the long term, it's really hard to work out how to be focused in the short term.

One of the difficulties of applying clear focus is that there will undoubtedly be conflict about what to focus on. The effective use of focus, therefore, almost always implies the effective resolution of conflicts. Typically, people who are not good at focusing are also not good at facing up to and resolving conflicts in a way that leaves the organization and the participants stronger. We all know about win/lose, but the really great producer of focus finds ways to make win/win outcomes the norm so that everyone can agree on what the critical few should really be.

The other aspect of this skill is that sometimes the critical few need to change – priorities shift, leaders alter their influence. At this point the highly skilled leader will be able to help colleagues and staff review their priorities and re-evaluate their focus. People can't just be told what to focus on, they need to do this evaluation for themselves. It can be a lengthy process and may seem to be a waste of time given the competition and all the other pressing matters that managers must attend to. But being focused is one of the keys to making a fast-moving organization work.

A lesson that is emerging from some of the fastest-moving internet businesses is that you make your decisions, move on, and don't worry if some of your decisions turn out to be wrong. Internet businesses seem to be in a continual state of experimentation. You take a view, you take an option, you make a decision, and if it doesn't work out, you're moving so quickly that as long as you learn from your failed decisions, no major damage will have been done. Life is exhilarating in these businesses. It's also very good if the stock price continues to rise and the value of the good decisions outweighs the cost of the bad ones. Is it the right approach? Probably it's the only approach for a fast-moving organization in a chaotic and shifting market. But the issue is not really the focus, the issue is the speed at which the focus is applied. When Time Warner and AOL merged in 2000, it was after Time Warner had tried to set up an internet activity which by most accounts had not succeeded. Time Warner was seen as a bureaucratic organization by the people from AOL. No doubt AOL was seen as quick, nimble and somewhat off-the-wall by some of the Time Warner inhabitants. But there was no question that both companies had grown because of clear market focus. They both knew how to apply themselves in the short and the long term. The difference seemed to be the speed at which they applied their decisions to fulfill their focus.

Links with other Enablers

We have already said that to be really focused you have to be able to cope with conflicts. So it is likely that the skills of selling change will be very useful (*see* p. 96). It will probably also be important to be able to convey shifts in focus cleanly and quickly to everyone involved and therefore the skills of the Simplifier will become premium at times (*see* p. 103). Can the overfocused prevent people enjoying their work? Yes, of course. Once you fall over the boundary from focused into obsessive, it is easy to lose sight of other people's needs and different motivations. Examples of organizations that have been focused and enthusiastic include The Body Shop in the UK and Southwest Airlines under Herb Keller. These were places where it was fun, to be focused and we all saw the great business results that emerged. The test for all leaders is when times get tough and focus is needed as much as fun. It is up to the leader to maintain motivation.

How to be better focused

1.   We should warn the reader that this is one of the toughest exercises in the book. Doing what we are about to suggest is

difficult for many people and produces results that many find discouraging. So *do not* go beyond this point unless you are ready to face up to these difficult, but fascinating results.

What we would like you to do is to analyze how you spend your time. We expect many of you have tried this already and know how tedious it is. We don't have a cure for that, except to say that this is slightly different as an exercise because we want you to analyze your time as you spend it on your *objectives* rather than on your *tasks*. So identify the key objectives that you have been trying to work on for a certain time period. Choose something at least a month long as your preferred time period. Now draw up a chart where you can analyze the amount of time you have cumulatively spent working on each of those priorities over the assigned period. At the end of the recording period, work out what proportion of your *total* working time you've spent on your top five priorities. *Health warning: This can be very depressing.* If the percentage goes below 50, then ask yourself, "Am I devoting enough time to my priorities and do I believe in my priorities?"

2.   Go back over a project that you have recently completed and pretend that you can rewind time. How would you reinvest your time with the benefit of hindsight? Remember, life is lived forward but understood in reverse.[21] Go over some of the significant stages of the project and how long you spent. Work out what you would do now. See if you can draw some general lessons on how you tackle projects in the future.

3.   We're going to give you this one as time off. We think that the two exercises above are both so powerful and so exhausting that you deserve a little break. Have this one on us!

Explore and expand

- When Phil was researching for his book, *What Do High Performance Managers Really Do,*[22] he discovered that all of us seem to rewrite our histories in terms of much greater focus after the event. Convince yourself that you may not be as focused as you believe you are, and go and seek other people's views about your ability to focus.

- Try to use one of the two recording techniques we've described above. You'll never know unless you get some quality data just how focused or not you really are.

- Sometimes you have to step back to lean forward. It may be easy to get focused on detail and forget that you could be focused on the big picture as well. Is the scope of your focus pitched at the right level?

Notes

20. Baylis, T. (1999) *Clock This*. London: Headline. *See abo* Smith G. (1999) "What makes him tick?" *Sunday Times*, September 12. London.

21. This is a rough paraphrase from Soren Kierkegaard (1813–55), a Danish philosopher and religious writer. He is seen as a precursor to twentieth-century Existentialism and a major influence on modern Protestant theology.

22. Hodgson P. and Crainer S. (1993) *What Do High Performance Managers Really Do?* London: Pitman Publishing.

CHAPTER 4

WHAT ARE RESTRAINERS?

Restrainers are negative or overplayed sides of those skills we call Enablers. While we have seen that Enablers help you get to where you need to be in handling ambiguity, Restrainers hold you back. They are behaviors and anti-skills that get in the way of effectively handling ambiguity and uncertainty. They prevent you from relaxing. With Enablers the more you do, the greater your ability to cope with uncertainty. But with Restrainers, the more you do the less well you handle uncertainty. We have found that many people have a particular blockage in coping with uncertainty that has been caused by one or possibly two specific Restrainers. If you can identify the particular Restrainer that is in your way and eliminate it or its effects, you can potentially make a great leap forward in relaxation – and thereby your ability to deal with uncertainty.

In all other respects, we've treated Restrainers in the same format and in the same style as Enablers.

> Restrainers are negative or overplayed sides of those skills we call Enablers.

How can I find out how well I am doing?

Use the checklists in each Enabler and Restrainer section. (For a more detailed and scientific measure, refer to The Ambiguity Architect.™ See reference note 1 on page 51.) Go through the areas you feel you most need to develop as Enablers and cut back as Restrainers. Then go through the checklist again, perhaps a month or two later. It is particularly useful to have one or two colleagues who are prepared to give you feedback on what they have seen. Bear in mind that behavior is what you actually do, not what you intend to do. You can't get much more practical than behavior.

HAVING TROUBLE WITH TRANSITIONS

The interval between the decay of the old and the formation and establishment of the new constitutes a period of transition which must always necessarily be one of uncertainty, confusion, error, and wild and fierce fanaticism.

John C. Calhoun (1782–1850)

Current thinking suggests that if you averaged all the things done in a day, the length of time most senior managers spend on dealing with each item is between seven to nine minutes per interaction. (Henry Mintzberg first documented this in 1979 in *The Nature of Managerial Work*.[1]) That means that in the average executive's day, they may switch between 60 to 80 different subjects, topics or problems. It wouldn't be so bad if each of these subjects were all of a similar type, but they are not. Hard or soft, long-term or short-term, external or internal – you are continually being put under a different spotlight each time. Your ideas, your memory, your capacity for compromise – from moment to moment you are required to switch between different, even opposite ways of behaving. The roller coaster continues, hardly ever stopping, seldom slowing down. How do you cope with this continual wild ride? If the answer is, "not well," then you might have a tendency to be *a Poor Transitioner*.

What problems will being a Poor Transitioner bring me?

To answer that question, let's look at the two major shifts that have occurred in organizations in the last few years.

More messages

The number of ways that people can communicate with you and others has increased enormously. An informal survey of a multinational electronics and engineering company showed that its senior managers were receiving between 40 and 80 e-mails per day, every day. In addition, they handled somewhere between 15 and 50 voicemail messages per day and that was not counting the phone calls where they actually connected with the person they wished to speak to. They also organized conference calls, face-to-face meetings, one-to-one discussions, and even wrote and received messages in script on good old-fashioned paper. Today, you could add texts, tweets, Slack messages, etc. Without doubt, the manager is bombarded with messages, communications, and requests in greater numbers than ever before. And from greater numbers of people representing diverse constituencies – inside and outside the organization.

More stuff

The downsizings, outsourcings, mergers, reengineering, and acquisitions of the recent past have now resulted in the managerial job that typically carries a lot more responsibility over a much broader area than ever before.

> Poor Transitioners often find shifting modes of behavior difficult.

You're responsible for more stuff now than you were ten years ago, and if you managed through the last decade, you will know that very well. More stuff translates into a greater variety of problems and issues. If you're just rising through the ranks, you may not know any different, but all the signs suggest that more stuff is on the way. The need is for you to be able to smoothly switch from a direct report with a problem customer, to a review of financial data, to a request for help with a new project, to a complaint about a new service, to ... and that was while you just walked down the corridor to get a cup of coffee!

One of the areas that Poor Transitioners often find most difficult is in shifting modes of behavior. You have a tough negotiation with a customer who is using all the tricks of the negotiating trade on you to beat your prices down. It's an exhausting meeting and tempers are getting pushed to the limit. But your next appointment is a sensitive one-on-one coaching talk with a key member of your staff whose wife is very ill and whose current poor performance is acting as a bottleneck and affecting the output of your entire team. How do you switch from tough and robust to sensitive and supportive?

Poor Transitioners are ...

Poor Transitioners have trouble shifting from one kind of task or one type of behavior to another. They prefer to use the same style for every activity.

Signs of Poor Transitioners

Tell-tale signs

- Their staff avoid going to them after certain kinds of meetings/events because they know that at that time their problem won't be handled with the requisite sensitivity.

- Hang on to certain projects too long and conversely push away or even ignore other projects of similar significance.

- Are known for being really good at some situations – for example, being friendly and supportive – but no one has ever seen them being tough and pushy (or vice versa).

- Show their lack of confidence in certain tasks.

- Are much better at either input or output, e.g. talking rather than listening or questioning rather than explaining.

Tell-tale actions

- Deal with all aspects of an issue before moving on.

- Only seem to ask the same questions, whatever the issue, i.e. "How are the numbers?" or "How long before it's finished?"

- Use the "one style fits all" approach.

Tell-tale phrases

- "I'm sorry, I'm too busy at the moment," and the moment seems to last forever.

Case study

The case of the unavailable executive

"Well, you'll just have to wait." The ringing and somewhat righteous tones of Muriel, the executive secretary to Systems Director Mike Allen, rang down the corridor. "But we must see Mike – it's very urgent," complained Bob, a software engineer. "Well, I'm sorry, he can't be disturbed at the moment. You know how he doesn't like to be interrupted when he's working on a position paper," Muriel responded.

Bob tried reasoning with Muriel. He told her she didn't understand, he argued and pushed, and finally he took his life in his own hands and insisted that he see Mike straight away. He pushed his way cautiously through into the inner office. Mike did not look at all pleased. His brow furrowed and in the coldest of tones, he asked Bob to explain why he had burst in on him. Bob was in a fix and he knew it. He'd discovered that the launch of a new product that was to be announced by the divisional chief executive contained a hardware fault and would not run properly. The options were to delay the launch – not good news – or to expensively work up a patch component and courier it to all distributors. Either action was well out of Bob's league, both in terms of authorizing the expense and in terms of handling the politics. Bob's own boss was away so he just had to speak to Mike.

Mike had been happily doing what he liked doing best: putting together a long-term scenario for the future of his part of the organization. He was very good at it, he enjoyed doing it and everybody said how well he did these kinds of things. He hated being interrupted and he hated even more being put on the spot by Bob with a crisis. Everybody knew he didn't do crises at all. Mike started to look for someone to blame and fired a few shots at Bob. It was Bob after all who had interrupted his brilliant train of thought and generally ruined his afternoon. After some terse and discouraging words, Mike sent Bob away saying that he needed time to think. But

Mike couldn't concentrate. His thoughts just didn't want to deal with the crisis. He wanted to be back in his secure world. In his terseness with Bob, he'd completely missed one important point, which was that the CEO was launching the product on the East Coast – three hours ahead of their own time zone. By the time Mike came out of his reverie an hour later, the CEO was just walking up to the podium to start his speech. It was going to be a bad month ...

How to become better at managing transitions

1.   Because this is a skill, it can be developed through practice, practice, and more practice. The best way to practice this skill is not to have the shift of transition forced on you, but to choose it yourself. So as you plan your list for today, look to see if you can make some deliberate shifts in style. Also see if you can shift from some projects and problems to others. Check whether in looking at problems or projects you make the assumption that your standard behavior is all that is required to solve the problem. Test yourself by the degree of shift you can cope with and little by little push up the extent of the shift – but each time under your own control. After doing this for a week or two, review how you are progressing. Then the difficult part – ask other people how they think you are doing.

2.   It may also be that your confidence to tackle the shift may not be as high as it could be. So once you've practiced the shifting kinds of projects as described above, try to organize a mix of items where you have different confidence levels. It may be that you have quite a high capability, but you aren't confident enough in applying your skills.

Try to swap between items and between skill confidence levels. Do something where you are confident of getting it done well and then immediately switch to something where you are not so confident. Now switch back to something where you have high confidence again. As always, review what you have learned from the process and see if you can figure out how to increase your confidence levels with some of the tasks and modes in which you need to operate.

Explore and expand

- Try to get the whole thing into perspective, and find out how significant your transition skills or lack of them really are. First, compare yourself with others, look carefully at the way they shift from level to level, mode to mode and see if you can do the same. Second, and most important, find out other people's views on how you operate. Much of this is perception, linked to skill and capability. Find out how people rate you.

- When you're reviewing your day, your week or your month, look for examples where an ability to switch from one problem/project to another would have been really useful and where it didn't matter much. Only focus on those areas where it matters.

- Note times when the transitions are difficult. Is it when there is a big risk? When you have to be future-oriented? Or is it some other thing? Sometimes we avoid or fail to make transitions when we are lacking in confidence about our ability to handle a specific type of situation.

Note

1.   Mintzberg, H. (1973) *The Nature of Managerial Work*. New York: Longman.

RESTRAINER 2

NOT MOTIVATED BY WORK

*Basically, I no longer work for anything but the sensation
I have while working.*

Albert Giacometti, sculptor (1901–66)

Are you a Wet Blanket?

'*I remember this company when we were at the top. We had the largest market share in most of our significant product ranges and we were the industry leader. People looked up to us. Now we are just waiting for the take-over offer that pleases the shareholders. Sometimes my job just seems to be helping banks make lots of money on us.*

The speaker isn't a fool and has been highly motivated in the past. But his company has managed to ignore the signs that the markets have been sending that its products and services are losing out to more aggressive and younger competitors. Little by little, the speaker and other employees have become more depressed with work. Work just isn't as much fun for him anymore, nor for anybody else who works with him. His behavior doesn't help either. Whereas once he was energetic and motivated, now everything is an effort. Once problems represented opportunities and invigorating challenge, now problems seem more like punishments visited on him by the "gods of business." He resents the intrusion that these problems bring and their disruptive effect on his otherwise harmonious life. In short, he has become a **Wet Blanket**.

Wet Blankets aren't born, they are created – and usually for one of broadly three reasons. The first and the most common route is where work was once exciting and interesting and now for a variety of reasons, it's not.

The second reason is where the skills and competencies the person has, which were once valuable and useful in the organization, are now superseded and so much less highly valued. Think of the technical expert who has not kept up their expertise with the latest developments, the practitioner whose skills have been overtaken by newer technology, or the salesperson whose best and most lucrative contacts have mostly retired or moved on. These are all people who once were motivated by work but now have become Wet Blankets.

The third example is only a part-time Wet Blanket. This is the person who is motivated only by a crisis and a drama. When there isn't such excitement going on, they become a part-time Wet Blanket and this state lasts until the next crisis looms. After a time, their colleagues begin to suspect that possibly they create a crisis just to make life more interesting and liven things up a bit.

> Wet Blankets aren't born, they are created.

Apart from making themselves miserable and unproductive, Wet Blankets can easily have the same downbeat effect on everyone they meet and work with. This can be particularly damaging if the Wet Blanket is a senior figure who may have been looked upon as a role model by a more impressionable junior member of staff. Wet Blankets can be the reason that the best and most talented people – the high potentials – move on from that area to get away from the negative emotion and seek out a place where there's more fun to be had.

Wet Blankets are ...

Wet Blankets have lost the ability to find work fun and energizing. They appear bored with their own work and negative toward other people's efforts. They smother enthusiasm by their negativity.

Signs of Wet Blankets

Tell-tale signs

- Seldom have a good word to say about the company, its products or its people.
- While not always critical of others, they may be very unsupportive.

- Possibly come alive in a crisis.
- Other staff work around them and seldom invite them on to their teams.
- Have no energy for work-related matters.

Tell-tale actions

- Save a lot of energy for things outside work.
- Don't smile much at work.
- Express little optimism for the future.
- Talk about how things once were or how they should be now. They don't appear to accept the present as it is and work towards a better future, i.e. they do not look for ways to enliven work. (*See* Exciter on p. 81.)

Tell-tale phrases

- "Is that the best they can do?" (said all the time about every result, every meeting).
- "Would you look at what those fools in marketing (or accounts, operations, human resources, head office, anywhere) have done now?"
- "What do you expect with top management like ours?"
- "This used to be a good company. I can't believe we've made these decisions."

Case study

The case of the miserable medic

Johannes, known to everyone as 'Old J,' is a 52-year-old medical doctor by training and a biomedical researcher by career orientation. He sat at his desk and frowned. He was good at frowning – his staff said behind his back that he practiced frowning for at least eight hours a day! He never looked interested, he never looked happy and, at work, he looked older than his years. The long-service workers who had known him earlier in his career said that he had not always been like that. He used to be exciting and energetic, but that was some time ago. Younger members of the firm were amazed if they happened to bump into him outside work on the ski slopes, where he was still an energetic enthusiast. To discover him laughing and joking with his friends and family was a shock! Far fewer people were privileged to hear him play the Beethoven piano sonatas for which he had an enormous and lifelong passion. None of this energy, none of this passion was now seen at work or had been seen for many years.

Johannes had received a message about a replacement member of staff he had requested from the HR department. He was puzzled, as he had asked for a mature person, not the youngster they seemed to have foisted on him. "She won't be of much use to us," he was thinking to himself. "Scarcely out of college, she'll be babbling with all the latest research theories and won't have the slightest skill worth talking about in real laboratory research. I don't know why I bother to ask HR."

Ann-Marie, aged 26 (first degree in bioengineering and biochemistry with three years industrial experience and an MBA from an international business school), had heard of 'Old J' and wondered what he would really be like. She had heard about the several product innovations which had emerged from his brilliant research in his younger days; how in his youth he worked with a team that were among the brightest sparks in his field ever to be seen in Europe; and had heard the whispered rumor that he'd been tipped for a Nobel, but a bigger name and a bigger laboratory in the US had received it that year. Some people said he had a grudge, others said it was just senility. No one said he was fun to work with. She wondered how she would cope.

We interrupt this narrative to point out that you already know the outcome of this story... This isn't Hollywood. After 9 tortured months, Ann-Marie starts looking for another job. At the exit interview with a sympathetic HR person, she explains she is leaving to work for an invigorating manager in a rival company. The HR person conducts a major review with Johannes and examines the effect he is having on his colleagues. He is made redundant and his entire team is reallocated. The HR department discovers that Ann-Marie was the third bright person that 'Old J' had lost for the company.

There's a two-part moral to this story. The first is that becoming a Wet Blanket is usually not a single-step process. It is easy to glide along a downward spiral over a number of years without realizing what is happening to you and what effect you are having on other people. Second, Wet Blankets are as much a danger to themselves as to their organizations. They reduce morale in general and can lose organizations key people whose potential may then be lost forever. But no one goes to work to be a Wet Blanket – it creeps up on them. So, what can be done?

How to throw off the Wet Blanket

1. Have you unwittingly slipped into "Wet Blanketdom"? Imagine you were trying to demotivate everyone in your office. What would you say? What would you do? Write down as long a list as you can imagine. Now review the list and ask yourself very seriously, do you ever catch yourself even slightly sounding like that or doing those things? If so, how can you work at removing those thoughts and activities from your daily work? It's not normally that difficult. Put the list in your pocket and at the next staff meeting, ask if you ever do any of these things *or* how often you do these things. Can you identify what you think causes you to be that way or do those things? Figure it out and remove the negative stimulus.

2. Is it the tasks or is it the overall motivation? If it's a task, then choose a task that you find a bit boring and ask your colleagues, or even better your children, how you could make it less boring. Take their advice. Even if it sounds silly, do what they suggest. Try it out and see whether it works.

3. If it's the overall motivation, you are like Johannes in our story but you haven't been made redundant yet. Take yourself for a walk and re-examine what your life is about and why you go to work. Why did you first come to work here? You will probably need some external help with this process – a coach or a mentor or a very good friend – or possibly all three. Talk these things through and get professional advice. HR can often be helpful in this respect. See if you can find a way to reinvigorate yourself as you reinvigorate your own job. Think of it this way: you really have very little to lose – if you don't give it a go you will never know. Otherwise, we're sorry to say, we think your fate will be similar to that of Johannes.

Explore and expand

There is only one step here – act now! What blankets are a danger to themselves and their organization, and therefore most organizations will not tolerate the negative impact that they have. Before you do anything more, if you think you are a Wet Blanket, stop reading this book and organize a conversation with someone whose views you respect. Ask this person how other people see you and how motivating you are to work with. Do people fight to join your group, or is your department seen as the 'Siberia' of the organization? You may not want to ask these questions and you certainly may not want to hear the answers. But look at what the real-life options are. Do you want to end up like Johannes?

RESTRAINER 3

FEAR OF CONFLICT

When I look back on all the worries I remember the story of the old man who said on his deathbed that he had a lot of trouble in his life, most of which never happened.

Winston Churchill (1874–1965)

Do you avoid conflict?

If you answered "yes," then you're in the majority. This is our most often encountered restrainer. Why? Apart from dealing with a subordinate performance problem, many managers will tell you that resolving conflict is their least favorite aspect of the managerial task. Most would privately argue that conflict is to be avoided rather than encouraged. In organizations that continually renew themselves, conflict is endemic. However, when conflict is handled effectively, it is much more likely to be around ideas rather than people.

Conflict-Avoiders don't want to get involved in disputes, especially when these disputes become full of emotion. Conflict-Avoiders usually find that conflicts between people and personalities are harder to handle. Conflict of ideas can often be settled by appealing to the logic of the situation or some expert advisor. But what if the idea is identified with the person?

We quite often coach entire top business teams to help them work better together. It never fails to amaze us how creatively a basic dispute between two or more powerful people can be maintained. The dispute can continue through any number of meetings and any number of apparently separate factual disagreements, sometimes for years. In fact, we have encountered several team projects where the real issue is not the team, but two or three people central to the team who can't get along. The chair of the meeting typically seems to be unwilling to remind both disputants that their unwillingness to find a way to agree – or at least respect each other's opinions – is costing the rest of the meeting its two most valuable resources, i.e. time and ideas. For a conflict of ideas to be healthy and to lead to some improved outcome, we believe that the two or more parties to the dispute must respect each other, even if they don't like each other.

So the task the Conflict-Avoider takes on is not to get the disputing parties to behave in a likable way, but to get them to declare their respect for the other members of the group and their agreement with the group's overall values and purpose. We would argue that if a member of a senior management team can't do this in the first place, they shouldn't be in senior management!

> Conflict-Avoiders have trouble dealing with heated situations and may be seen as too accommodating to others.

Conflict-Avoiders find themselves torn between two possibilities. They want to stay on good terms with their people – after all, who knows when they might need some help or a favor themselves? But they also need to create the conditions of change – which not everybody likes and which will rub at least some colleagues the wrong way. These are also issues of risk and focus. To what extent is the Conflict-Avoider prepared to risk being seen as the 'bad cop' who is out of step? And to what extent is the Conflict-Avoider prepared to keep focused on the current issue? Could they themselves be accused of stirring up conflict? Or could they be accused of becoming obsessive about the problem? Sometimes conflict, or at least open disagreement, is a necessary stage on the road to solving a problem.

There are also huge potential cultural differences between what is acceptable discussion and debate in one culture and what is seen as negative conflict in another. We have worked with the senior team of a Swedish company that had been acquired by a US corporation. The team was made up roughly of half Swedes and half Americans. We worked with the team through a strategy workshop to resolve some major issues. In the pre-workshop phone interviews, most of the Americans talked about wanting to bring conflict out into the open, while most of the Swedes talked about wanting to resolve their problems in a productive way. At the workshop itself, when one of the Americans talked about encouraging conflict during the two days, a couple of the Swedes visibly winced. In their view, conflict was only one stage away from open fist-fighting. For the Americans, the same word meant a good debate where everyone aired their views clearly. The misplaced use of just one word could have ruined the two-day meeting. Fortunately, by understanding the cultural differences in the use of that one word, everyone was able to work together to achieve what they all wanted – the start of better communication that would lead to a resolution and positive agreement over the strategic way forward.

Conflict-Avoiders are ...

Conflict-Avoiders have trouble dealing with heated situations and may be seen as too accommodating to others.

Signs of Conflict-Avoiders

Tell-tale signs

- Staff may moan to them about their problems with others, but nothing gets done.

- Dislike people getting emotional and hate tears and squabbling.

- Won't tackle a personal disagreement that simmers on and on.

- Won't call people to order.

Tell-tale actions

- Don't get involved in disputes.

- Won't tell people to stop arguing among themselves.

- Give in to the person who makes the strongest protest.

- Listen too much and consequently hear the same story more than once.

- Confuse a debate about personality with a debate about ideas.

Tell-tale phrases

- "I don't want to play God."

- "They're adults, can't they settle it themselves?"

- "People are allowed to have strong opinions. That's healthy, isn't it?"

- "I don't understand what all the fuss is about."

- "I wish those two would get along better."

Case study

The case of the conflict-wary chief

Misha was worried. He had just spent 30 minutes with Lars, his brilliant vice-president of marketing whom he had managed to lure away from the competition only 12 months ago. Lars had spent the entire time telling him in very clear language that if he didn't do something about his chief finance officer Bernard, then Lars was going to think seriously about whether he really wanted to see his long-term career future with Misha's company. Misha sighed. He hated it when two people he liked, trusted, and valued were at each other's throats. Worse still, he could see each person's point of view. Of course, Bernard wanted to keep costs down and get clear forecasts for spending. Equally important was Lars's insistence on flexibility to pursue opportunities as they emerged, especially as nowadays e-business opportunities came out of the gate very fast indeed.

Misha knew it was a problem that as CEO he ought to do something about, but he didn't know how and if the truth were really told, he felt uncomfortable about playing God. He began to dread the next top management meeting. Lars and Bernard were sure to fight, and if they didn't, they'd be stiffly polite to each other. They probably wouldn't contribute anything useful to the meeting and would make everyone else at the table feel uncomfortable and unprepared to contribute ideas. They would pull down the entire team's performance and ideas were definitely what were needed at the moment, since the organization was facing some major challenges from the competition. The board needed to lead the way, rather than wasting its time taking trivial shots at each other. Soon, Misha knew, his other directors would be coming to him privately and saying he must do something about the problem. If Lars or Bernard had to go, then so be it, but the organization couldn't afford to be placed in a state of limbo because of this continuing dispute.

Oh, what to do? Misha was just about to summon up the courage to call Lars and Bernard into his office when the phone rang. Misha heaved a sigh of relief – it was something he could understand and could tackle. He'd shelve the Lars/Bernard dispute for another hour or two ...

How conflict avoidance reduces effectiveness

Any organization that is coping with continual change – and show us one that isn't – will need to face up to conflict. The resolution of different ideas, of different approaches, or of different styles will all contribute to the way a company reshapes and renews itself on a continual basis. Therefore, every manager – we would go further, every participant – in that organization needs to be able to step up to conflict and dispute. To do this effectively they need to have the skills and the confidence to resolve it in such a way that the outcome improves the quality of the organization, improves the bonding of the team, and produces outputs and results that are of positive use to the organization. The key to this in our view is to not confuse personality and ideas. There can be enormous room to express ideas in different ways and different styles, but the idea is still basically the same. If the debate is around how to make use of that idea, then the conflict can be quite intense during the period of resolution, without it affecting the relationships of the individuals. The prerequisite for all this to occur positively is trust and respect between all the parties. Therefore, the person with final responsibility for resolving disputes is the one who has to ensure that every member of that dispute shows appropriate respect and also contributes 100 percent to the overall aim of that group. The group can be a small project team, or it can involve thousands of workers in an organization.

How to reduce your aversion to conflict

1. A lot is known about handling conflict. There are professionals in it. The customer-contact people in hotels and airlines should have been trained to a very high level. Next time you are making a booking or checking into an airport, see how the professionals

handle the conflicts and handle the needs of the customer. You'll notice that they distinguish between the message and the emotion. See if you can do the same. When you are faced with a particular conflict, see if you can extract the emotion and put it to one side and look at the intention. What is the intention of each party? Can that be used positively to ensure that there is a greater level of agreement?

2. First of all, practice using these skills at the lowest level. If there is a minor tiff in a meeting you are running, use the same technique. Ask for feedback later from both (or all) participants.

3. Watch for the emotion in yourself. If you are getting emotionally involved in the dispute, then you will be less able to keep a clear head to resolve it in the best way. Get some feedback from colleagues about how easily your emotions are triggered. Recognize those triggers have taken some while to be created and set up a plan for the next six months to gradually give you back control over your emotions.

Explore and expand

- Make a list. How many conflicts and disputes are still outstanding? How many are still in your inbox as disputes unresolved?

- Choose the simplest dispute and call together both parties. Establish that they both have the same intention and then insist they work it out then and there in front of you.

- When a dispute occurs in a meeting you are running, force yourself to say how pleased you are that this has occurred. Check with each of the disputants that they want to resolve it publicly and to the best advantage of the organization. Then set a time limit and let them get on with it.

INTRODUCTION TO
RESTRAINERS 4 AND 5

Make everything as simple as possible, but not simpler.
Albert Einstein (1879–1955)

Who did you confuse today – yourself or someone else?

We use words as stepping stones to:

1. progress our own understanding by thinking in words. By hopping from one stepping stone word to the next, we progress through a thought pattern. Humans have been doing this from the beginning of time.

2. trigger similar thoughts in others by the use of those same words. When I say "beach" to you, we have similar ideas triggered in our minds – sea, sand and waves, etc. Of course, to be pedantic, if I'd wanted to convey "beach in the Arctic Ocean," you probably would have to reevaluate your thoughts. But essentially, we use words to trigger thoughts in others similar to the thoughts we have ourselves.

    Restrainers 4 and 5 are both about confusion. Restrainer 4 is about being internally confused and Restrainer 5 is about confusing others. We've treated them separately because people often suffer from only one. However, they are both caused by lack of clarity. It is our belief that the pursuit of clarity is a skill and can be learned.

RESTRAINER 4

MUDDY THINKING

The English never draw a line without blurring it.

Winston Churchill (1874–1965)

You may be confusing yourself

Have you ever worked with someone who never seemed to fully under-stand exactly what was going on? It was as if they understood 80 percent of a problem but never quite put *all* the pieces into place. They seemed internally confused, and they didn't appear to have a fundamental grasp of how things worked. When they tried to discuss the problem with you, they didn't know what to do about it – or as it were, which levers to pull. You were dealing with a **Muddy Thinker**.

Muddy Thinkers make problems more difficult to solve and concepts more difficult to understand. They do this to themselves, but there is a danger that when they open their mouths they can do it to others, too. They use their thoughts and their language loosely and ambiguously. They are not precise and they don't anchor their meaning to specific words. The result is they are not clear to themselves and often not clear to others. As you hear them talk about a subject, you get a sensation that they are reporting everything third- or fourth-hand, that they don't really have a good grasp of what they are describing. In their minds nothing is stable or thoroughly understood.

However, Muddy Thinkers may sometimes appear to be clear. This is the most dangerous variety. They speak clearly and they use simple words, but you later discover that they heard them all from someone else.

They were just repeating things without understanding them. In their own heads, they were not at all clear. The evidence is when you try to explore the possibilities or the "what-ifs?" of a situation with them. They have no conceptual apparatus in their heads, no models or constructs they can play with to model the situation and come up with possible outcomes.

Muddy Thinkers are ...

Muddy Thinkers confuse themselves and others by making simple issues more complex and less precise.

Signs of Muddy Thinkers

Tell-tale signs

- Lack clarity of thought.
- Don't appear to have a clear understanding of what they want to do.
- Don't know how things work.
- Have no fundamental grasp of what is going on.
- Don't care how things work.

Tell-tale actions

- Confuse one concept with another.
- Describe what happens, but not why it happens.
- Are not precise.
- Don't extrapolate from existing understanding.
- Don't know which levers to pull.
- Are poor at forecasting – guess a lot.
- Confuse themselves and others before anything is well understood.

Tell-tale phrases

- "I hadn't really thought about it like that."

- "I'm not sure I fully understand this."

- "Isn't everything so confusing now?"

- "I'm sure it will all turn out to be much simpler than it looks."

- "Gosh, I never realized that."

Case study

The start-up that got lost in the fog

It's easy to think that students and young people are taking over the entire business world. Young people in the new sciences seem to be able to pull off miracles in new business start-ups. If the business press is to be believed, they are doomed to succeed in almost every case. Well, to redress the balance a tiny bit, here's the story of a start-up that didn't actually make it.

Meet two students. Micky Mudd, known to one and all as Muddy, first met Clare O'Flarity, known as Clarity, when they were finishing an MBA course at a US university. Muddy was great on ideas and big picture opportunities. He showed enormous, boundless enthusiasm for future ideas and would work on them with an energy and drive that was truly amazing. He was never very good at being precise and when questioned about his big picture visions, he was never very clear on the details on how they would work out. But that never stopped his enthusiasm. Clarity, on the other hand, was not so good with the big ideas, but was very good at being clear and precise. She was never happy unless she had everything understood from the large right down to the small details. She wasn't worried whether the idea was an original one or one that other people felt could never happen. She just had to make sure she fully understood what was going on and had it clear in her own mind. Clarity and Muddy found they could work together very well and bring their opposite approaches together with positive effect for them both.

Like many of the students in their MBA years, they had an idea for a business. Unlike most of the other students, however, when they explained their idea to their professor, she got extremely excited and said she thought they had a real business opportunity. They tested their idea on several other professors at the university and many of the other students. Whenever they told their story, they got a lot of genuine and admiring interest. Everyone knew that Clarity and Muddy were going to become rich very soon.

After exams they arranged to convey their ideas to a venture capitalist. The big day dawned and unfortunately with it, so did a streptococcal infection of Clarity's throat. She couldn't speak. She had a temperature of 103° and she couldn't make the VC's meeting. Such was their enthusiasm for the project and their urgency to get going that they decided Muddy should make the presentation to the venture capitalist. Oh, what a mistake that was!

Muddy did his best to try to explain the concept of the business idea, the market, the way the idea was scalable to grow with time once they had established a core market. He used all the words that he had heard Clarity use when she described the project, but somehow in his hands the presentation didn't fly. The venture capitalist asked some good and some difficult questions and with each one Muddy waffled. It was clear before the meeting was over that the funding would not be theirs. The venture capitalist was impressed with Muddy's enthusiasm and zeal, but he really didn't go away from the meeting convinced, on the basis of what Muddy had said, that the two of them would be able to deliver a viable business product. He needed data, a clear understanding of what was being proposed, and a very clear sense that the future chief executive sitting in front of him knew exactly what he was talking about. He came away with none of these.

There is a sad ending to this story. Muddy didn't really understand why the venture capitalist had turned them down. He came away with the impression that the VC felt their ideas were no good and that it was pointless continuing looking for other VC's to fund them. As a result, Muddy and Clarity never pursued this business opportunity. They went on to live perfectly happy lives, of course, but the opportunity that could have been was lost simply through an inability to express an idea clearly.

Get rid of the mud!

1. Things are not clear; concepts are unstable. It seems all too easy not to understand something. If this is the case with you, start to work first on the words you use. Do some exercises – like scales on a piano – where you take a concept and try to describe it in no more than 25 words. Leave it for a short time and then go back and cut down the number of words you used. Choose several of the main projects that you're involved in at work. Try to describe

each of those to yourself in as few words as possible, not exceeding the magic 25. Now try out your descriptions on other people. Ask them for their suggestions. When somebody offers you a description of something, see if you can describe it back to them in fewer words than they used. Construct questions like "Is it like X?" to hone in on the description.

2. Muddy Thinkers often crowd their minds with lots of ideas and things so that they stumble around when trying to think clearly. As a different exercise, think each night before you go to sleep, "What is the one single thing I must achieve tomorrow that would make the greatest improvement?" Write down that single thing on a card and keep the card in front of you all the next day. Continue to try this process. Resist all temptation to have more than one item on the card. (You're allowed to do more than one thing in a day, but in terms of training your mind to think of one thing, this is the best way.)

Explore and expand

- You'll probably know if you get confused a lot, but maybe you work in a confusing industry. Before you go any further, check with some colleagues. Do they understand you or do they find you difficult to understand? Do they get the sense that you know what you're talking about? Or truthfully, do they think that you spend a lot of your time more confused than they do? We all have blind spots – this could be one of yours. Check first.

- If it looks like you may be more muddy than you thought, set aside some practice time for the enhancing exercises above. Remember, this is a skill. If you want to get better, you have to practice. The more you practice, the better you will become. Remember that most of your life you have been practicing what you are now, i.e. a Muddy Thinker. You need to unlearn and relearn. This takes time and can also be quite tiring.

- The early stages of learning this skill are often a chore. Find someone to help you, support you and give you encouragement and feedback. This could be a relative, a friend or a colleague. Find somebody as you start rather than when you're beginning to lose energy and enthusiasm.

RESTRAINER 5

COMPLEX COMMUNICATION

He can compress the most words into the smallest idea of any man I know.

Abraham Lincoln (1809–65)

Did you confuse someone else today?

In the previous section, we discussed what happens when a person does not use words clearly or reliably in their own thinking. The output is internal confusion, which we described as Muddy Thinking. In this section we are going to explore what happens when a person has clear enough thoughts in their own head, but can't find a way to let those thoughts escape into clear, simple and concise verbal descriptions for others to appreciate and understand. We call these people **Complex Communicators**.

The US Department of Justice Immigration and Naturalization Service form I-94W – non-immigrant visa waiver – needs to be completed by most non-US citizens on entry into the USA. Paragraph (c) begins

> *Have you ever been or are you now involved in espionage or sabotage; or in terrorist activities; or genocide; or between 1933 and 1945 were you involved, in any way, in persecutions associated with Nazi Germany or its allies?*

As legalese, it's fine, and one could argue at that level it has great precision. But for the ordinary traveler arriving in the United States for a short holiday, the question seems bafflingly complex and richly ironic. After all, if you were the sort of person involved in such activities, would you admit to it? We have heard it argued that the whole question could be summarized simply as "are you wanted for international crimes?" It sounded to us as if that question would get just as good an answer as the current lengthier one.

In this section, therefore, we are dealing with people who start off with a clear thought and then complexify it in such a way that other people understand the question less well or not at all. Here is a quote from the beginning of a report:

> *The proposals made in response to this request show differences of approach to the problem that relate to the differing recommendations of the Committee's report and includes some modifications of those recommendations.*[2]

What does that mean? The best we can guess is: "Here is the report." If you sometimes send messages like the example above, there is a danger that you are a Complex Communicator.

> It is easy to become a Complex Communicator.

We notice a worrying trend that as it becomes simpler to send more messages, the meaning and the clarity that goes with each message seems to get downgraded. It is easy to become a Complex Communicator. How many e-mails have you struggled through where a few words would have conveyed the message much better than the many you are forced to scan through?

Complex Communicators are ...

Rather than breaking down the complex into the simple in their explanations, Complex Communicators have the knack of building up the simple into the complex.

Signs of Complex Communicators

Tell-tale signs

- Don't take into account how much others do or do not understand.
- Don't check what people already know when preparing to give an explanation.

- Open their mouths before the thoughts have been arranged.

- Make assumptions that other people know what jargon words mean.

- Use confusing language to explain a simple idea.

- Use more words than necessary.

- Use longer words than necessary.

- Use jargon loosely and without precision.

Tell-tale actions

- Add irrelevant concepts.

- Do not unroll an explanation in a logical step-by-step way.

- Don't give people time to assimilate the explanation before moving on to the next part.

- Hop from subject to subject in explaining an idea, or spend a lot of time on one aspect but hardly any time on the other – for instance, 30 minutes describing an elephant's foot and 30 seconds describing the rest of its body.

- Ask a question and then qualify it and qualify it again.

- Make a statement, then qualify it, then qualify it again.

Tell-tale phrases

- "I'm sure you all know about the B530 upgrades, so I'll just go right ahead and talk about the latest developments," (to an audience that included people who didn't know what a B530 was).

- "The overall purpose of this project, well, that is, the new project, not forgetting the additional responsibilities that we've also taken on, and of course allowing for the current thinking from our research people, who by the way have just had some really good news. Did you all hear about that research?" (from the project leader to the project team on the first occasion they all met together).

Case study

Mr Plexs tries to improve road safety

Colin Michael Plexs – yep, you guessed it – known to his friends as Com-Plexs, recently had an unfortunate experience in his village. While trying to cross the road on a rather dangerous bend, he was nearly hit by a car that was going too fast. Being a man of action, he decided that something must be done. He decided clearly and resolutely that road safety must be improved in the village. But how to do it? Who should do it? What needed to be done? He also knew that he had to explain his ideas to everyone else in the village. So that evening he called together five of his closest friends and presented the problem to them. What he ought to have said was, "I was nearly knocked down by a speeding car today and I'm looking for ideas on how we can improve road safety in the village." Instead what he said was, "I was nearly killed today by a speeding car. I've been thinking about this for some time. The problem isn't a new one, it's been growing worse every day and we can't let it get any worse because we've all got children. And how is your daughter Jane, by the way? I've just heard from Felicity and she says that ... Anyway, back to the story. While I think the local authorities should be brought into this and we need someone to represent us, do you know anyone on the local town council, John? Otherwise, I wonder if we should write a letter to the newspaper and anyway this is all getting very worrying. We've all got children, after all."

He went on like this for some time. His friends listened patiently for as long as they could stand it and then John intervened. "So why did you bring us here tonight?" he asked. "Well, haven't I made myself plain?" asked Colin looking somewhat perplexed.

John and the others finally got out of Colin that he favored getting the roadway altered so that it forced cars and trucks to go slower around the dangerous corner. Although it would have been nice to have a bypass for the village, they all agreed that was unlikely at the present time. Under John's gentle guidance, an action plan was worked out. But what would have happened if Colin had been left to ramble?

How to make the complex seem simple

We quite often find that Muddy Thinking (*see* p. 145) and the Complex Communicator go hand-in-hand. However, it is quite possible for a person to have very clear thoughts without expressing them in a way that others can understand. The following suggestions are aimed at that category:

1. When you try to explain something to an audience, find out as much as you can about what the audience already knows – and what they need to know. Then pretend to listen through their ears to what you are saying. Would you understand what you were saying if you were hearing it for the first time?

2. When making an explanation, restrict yourself to a maximum of *five* points. Break down everything into five or fewer sections. Ideally, we would recommend you go for three sections, but some things do need a little more. Whatever it is you are trying to explain, start the sentence with, "This falls into three parts" (or five parts if you must).

3. You are working with one other person or a very small group of people. You need to describe a problem. Divide it into a few stages (no more than five) and then after each stage of your description, ask your audience to repeat back to you what they have understood, what the key points were, the areas of significance, and the action points that emerged. Of course, this will only work if you don't have a room full of other Complex Communicators! If you do this several times, you will soon learn how well your explanation transfers to other people. By inviting them to tell you what they remember, they're giving you the best feedback you can get about which parts of the explanation worked and which didn't.

Explore and expand

- Think of your managerial role as not only to do with decision making and communicating ideas, but also to do with simplifying. Search out areas of your own and, if you are brave, other people's work in which you can bring greater clarity. If you suspect you are a Complex Communicator, we have sympathy with you. Most things do seem more complex nowadays. Look for a few areas (no more than three) where the extra effort needed to turn a complex communication into one that's clear and simple is really going to pay off. For instance, would it help your people if you could explain the company strategy in less than 25 words?

- Look around your organization today at what is said and what is written. Look at your company mission statement, a statement on strategy, a quarterly internal report, or a selection of e-mails. How much do you live in a culture which encourages complexity? How much would simplicity be valued? Weigh these thoughts when thinking about how much effort you need to/want to put into this particular skill.

Note

2. Quoted by Sir Ernest Gowers in *The Complete Plain Words* (1987). London: Penguin.

INTRODUCTION TO RESTRAINERS 6 AND 7

Did I miss something?

In a world where Intel's previous CEO Andy Grove stated, 'Only the paranoid survive'[3] and where even Bill Gates said of Microsoft at the height of its powers that it should only anticipate six months' certainty of any market, it is clear that competition and change may come from any direction at any time – probably faster than you thought. If this is true, then to get too narrow in your thinking and too deep into the detail of the present may be a mistake for two reasons:

1. If your head is well down, then you may miss an important new piece of information that could significantly influence the way you do your business now or the way others compete with you. (See our book, *The Future of Leadership*, and *Scan ahead* on p. 62 of this book.)

2. If you focus too much on the detail, you'll miss the obvious larger picture and will probably reduce your flexibility.

We see narrowing your thinking and concentrating too much on the detail as Restrainers because of their impact on flexibility and vision. A dilemma is that sometimes the detail is crucially important and should not be ignored. While writing this book, the crisis about tire safety at Ford and Firestone came to mind. In various stories, it had been reported that the data existed – for at least two years – showing possible tire defects. Why didn't someone pay attention to the details? Why weren't the details pieced together to reach what are now considered obvious conclusions?

Note

3. Grove, A. (1999) *Only the Paranoid Survive: How to Exploit the Crisis Points that Challenge every Company*. Bantam Books.

RESTRAINER 6

HOOKED ON DETAIL

Not everything that can be counted counts, and not everything that counts can be counted.

Albert Einstein (1879–1955)

Could you be more precise, please?

Your people bring you an idea. What is your first response? Do you praise the breadth of their vision? (After all, you are supposed to be developing them to take on your role sometime soon.) Or do you point out the lack of solid information that backs it up and comment unfavorably about the way the spreadsheet and the graphical evidence is presented? If it's the second option, then you may be a **Detail Junkie**. Of course, if you are, then you'll want us to give you a lot more information to prove our assertion! One way you can get a lot more detail is by going through the tell-tale signs on p. 160. If you see yourself in at least 60 percent of the items there, then you should be concerned. Bear in mind that you may not think you are a Detail Junkie, but others might. They may be able to see what you cannot.

> Detail Junkies focus on the small matters often to the exclusion of the larger issues and the bigger picture.

"But the devil is in the detail," you might argue. "Someone needs to be concerned with the detail since if we get it wrong, our products and processes won't work properly, and we lose customers." We agree. But let us remind ourselves that this book is about coping with ambiguity and uncertainty. We've already identified that most organizations around the world face increasing levels of uncertainty and increasing speeds of operation. Given that scenario, how much time and energy can a company afford to put into unnecessary detail?

Let's be clear that there's detail, and then there's detail. If a company sells you a piece of software that keeps crashing and it doesn't have all the functions that it was advertised to have, then you are rightly critical of some level of detail in the design and output of the product. If, on the other hand, a perfectly serviceable piece of software is delayed to the market for so many months because someone keeps wanting to redesign the external packaging, there may be far less justification for concern over that kind of detail.

Our proposition is that in any project/product/process, there will be "essential detail" – detail that just *has* to be right for the thing to deliver its promises – and there will also be what we call "trivial detail." These may be nice to have or fun to do but in no way affect the speed, quality, cost of whatever the output is. The point is that Detail Junkies can't tell the difference between essential detail and trivial detail.

This knack of discrimination is going to cost you a lot if you are a Detail Junkie. Why? Because the time you should be spending on big ideas (and yes, we know that big ideas are often fuzzy at the edges and not detailed or precise enough) is the time you spend instead on trivial detail. How do you tell the difference between the essential and the trivial? At root it's in your attitude toward handling uncertainty. Consider these statements about attitude:

- "I look for the minimum detail necessary to understand enough about the project or item before moving on."

- "I feel I am progressively reducing uncertainty with the more detail about the project I can assimilate and the more detail I can include into the project, no matter what the detail relates to. For me, more detail equals more certainty."

If you prefer the first statement, then you can easily spot the trivial, because it gets in the way of the essential. However, if your preference tends toward the second statement (and we have made these two rather starkly different to demonstrate our point), then you embrace the trivial detail and at times might even be accused of wallowing in it.

Detail Junkies are ...

Detail Junkies focus on the small matters often to the exclusion of the larger issues and the bigger picture.

Signs of Detail Junkies

Tell-tale signs

- Have difficulty seeing the larger possibilities of an idea.
- See detail as the way to understand complexity and uncertainty.
- Try to achieve certainty through the small and the detailed.
- Tend to decide slowly and want to check all the data more than once.
- Seldom take a flier on an idea or a concept.
- Would rather be slow and precise than quick and approximate.

Tell-tale actions

- Frequently ask about the small matters, seldom about the large.
- Use a reductionist approach – the smaller it can be broken down, the more we can understand it.
- Allow themselves to be held back from the big picture by concentrating on the small.
- Avoid fuzzy descriptions and anything else that is imprecise.
- Read everything at least twice, no matter if it's important or not.
- Constantly spot typos and other small errors.
- Test the validity of an idea by questioning one aspect only, but in great depth.

Tell-tale phrases

- "Just tell me about the detail of that aspect again."
- "That sounds too vague to me. Can't you make that more precise?"
- "Haven't you got more information on this?"
- "Isn't sycophantic spelled with an F?"

Case study

The case of the unseen response

My boss Brenda is detail driven. Whenever you present an idea or a proposal to her, the first thing she comments on is some trivial aspect of the proposal that doesn't quite match up with something she had seen earlier. For instance, she'll comment on the alignment of columns that she didn't like. It's irritating but we get by. I know she learned to be this concentrated on detail when she was in my job and worked for a man who was exactly the opposite to herself. He didn't set the details clearly in anything and would expect everybody else to sort out the arrangements. Then he would expect them all to work perfectly, even though he had done nothing to contribute toward them. His contribution would be to change his mind several times along the way. Brenda got very good at details, to the extent that eventually, when her boss completely failed to see an important shift in the market (yes, it was a detail when it first emerged, but it was an important detail), he got fired and she was put into his place. The trauma of seeing her boss fired emphasized to Brenda even more significantly the importance of getting the detail right. She made our lives miserable at times because of this very reason. As a marketing colleague of mine used to say, "This is OK in peace time, but we're not fast enough for war."

And war it was. We were the largest of three major competitors in a key market and we were preparing for one of the major world conferences and exhibitions for our business area. With no warning, our two competitors announced that they were merging their previously competing divisions to form a new business. This caught analysts, ourselves and everybody else, by complete surprise. From being marginally the largest in the market, suddenly we were dealing with a single competitor that would be close to twice our size. The Asian exhibition and conference was due in two weeks and was going to be the place where everyone in the business wanted to find out what was really going on. They'd be asking what the newly merged organization was going to really look like and, most important from our point of view, how we were going to respond. The question we were facing was, how should we demonstrate to our existing customers that we were not being overshadowed by the new competitors? Could we use this as an opportunity to argue our strengths compared with the potential disruption the other two would be facing during their merger period?

Brenda had asked for ideas. Two colleagues and I brainstormed a number of ways we might modify our exhibition and conference presentations. We argued that as an integrated producer of several products, we were now offering a better range with greater interconnectivity than our confused competitors. We also wanted to bring forward the announcement of some American research and construct an outline of a new product – a concept product – that would revolutionize one aspect of the market. The product wouldn't be available for at least 12 months, but it would certainly capture the imagination of many people who would be visiting the exhibition and could be our strongest weapon in distracting our customers from our competitors' merger. Anyway, we argued that the IT and car markets were always producing beta-test versions and concept models, why couldn't we do it too?

The meeting with Brenda didn't go well. She was immediately cautious about our great ideas. Exactly what were we proposing? What detailed specification of the new product did we have? How much would it cost to make? How soon could we make it? How could we guarantee quality? What would happen to our existing products? On and on and on she went asking some very good questions, but also some very trivial ones. This would have been fine if we were going through a typical product launch procedure where we had a lot more room to debate these issues. But all of us were very aware that the exhibition was only a couple of weeks away and if we were going to make any kind of announcement, we had to start preparing it very soon. Again and again we explained that it was just a concept idea, something to prove that we had good ideas too and that we had a research program at least the equal of anything our competitors could put forward. But Brenda wasn't happy. She wanted so much detail and so much reassurance that the whole project was shelved.

In the end we did nothing. Our products were displayed as usual. Our sales and marketing lines were what everyone was expecting. We had nothing new to offer the conference or the exhibition. Our competitors, on the other hand, although they acknowledged they were in for an interesting time post-merger, could offer all kinds of opportunities and possibilities, which they did lavishly and winningly to their own customers and to many of ours too. They argued for the benefits of the merger and several of our existing customers came up to me on the exhibition stand and asked point blank what our response was going to be.

I don't know what our lack of response at that exhibition did to our market exactly, except that over the following 12 months our sales figures went down three percentage points compared with our competitors, who seemed to be increasing their share. I wouldn't have liked to have been in Brenda's shoes when she had her performance appraisal, but then I wasn't with the company anymore. The competition had offered me a better job and I joined them.

How to treat the Detail Junkie habit

1. The problem is likely to be in distinguishing the essential detail from the trivial. Conduct an historic survey. Review a project that you have already been involved in, whose outcome you already know. Examine now with the benefit of hindsight which areas of detail were crucial to the successful outcome of the project. Then review all the other areas where you asked for detail at the time, where later it became clear that the detail was insignificant to the proper functioning of the project. Can you spot any patterns? Can you see how you could have learned earlier the difference between the essential and the trivial?

2. When working with others, ask them how much detail they need. You may be surrounded by Detail Junkies or you may have a room full of "big picture" addicts. Either way, understand other people's points of view and then try to accommodate them.

3. Practice asking for the big picture first. And only after you have done that, allow yourself to get into the detail. Use stock phrases like "How does this fit into the bigger picture?" "What is its longer-term implication?" or "How would it affect our overall strategy or plans?" Use these phrases as the very first thing you ask and then allow yourself into the detail. Little by little you'll start to train yourself to focus on both the big and the small.

Explore and expand

-   Whenever you start to work with something, as a cautionary step, ask yourself, "If this didn't get done at all, what would be the long-term impact? How much would this piece of detail affect the overall spin of the planet?"

- Think about your role and how it is perceived by other people in the organization. Is your job one where detail is the main component, or are you expected to be able to see a broader strategic view as well? How much does your organization expect you to deal with detail? How much does it expect you to deal with a larger image? Having understood that, how much would it surprise people if you start to disregard the trivial and search only for the essential detail? Sometimes you need to gain permission from others in the organization to give you space to develop a new trivial, detail-free approach.

RESTRAINER 7

NARROW BAND THINKING

There is no reason anyone would want a computer in their home.

Ken Olsen, president, chairman and founder of
Digital Equipment Corporation, 1977

Why didn't I think of that?

Why make bendable electronics and flexible screens? Because if you could, you'd be able to wear your computer and fold up your display. These things might be tricky to make, because many of their components are based on silicon, which is a crystal, and crystals are hard and inflexible. Now the narrow route to the solution is to keep looking for bendable crystals. This has proven to be very elusive, but doable. Of course, things that are bendable like plastics would be wonderful if they could conduct electricity the way silicon does, but they don't. The nearest that's been achieved have performance levels far less effective than good old silicon. So what to do? The narrow approach is to keep bashing away at the silicon and hope that eventually you'll find some way of making crystals bend. But why don't we take a non-narrow approach? Why don't we blend crystals and plastics together, sort of like oil and water (or even better, like oil and ice cubes)? Trouble is, as we all know, they don't mix.

> Narrow Thinkers focus on the here and now and miss possibilities because of their "tunnel vision" approach.

So here's your narrow-band thinking test. Where might you look to find an example of plastic (think oil) and crystals (think ice) mixing? OK, thinking time's up. Well the answer is, in the blood of the Antarctic winter flounder, of course! What are we talking about? The Antarctic winter flounder's blood ought to freeze, given the habitat that it swims in, but it doesn't. This is because the flounder has evolved a way to suppress the formation of ice crystals in its blood. Its blood is full of oily compounds very similar to the plas-tics that computer people want to incorporate in their basic design. By studying how the Antarctic winter flounder stays alive by keeping its blood on the border between frozen and unfrozen, computer scientists may be able to formulate a bendable crystalline mix that will have a better performance than your current computer. Science fiction? Maybe in 1998 when it was part of a National Science Foundation $1.7 million award led by chemical engineer Paulette Clancy of Cornell University.[4] Clancy wanted to learn more about how silicon and polymers work together and that meant understanding the boundary where the two meet – a situation that the flounder deals with every day of its life.

Being a **Narrow Thinker** means you miss out on the unexpected links and the bringing together of ideas that would not otherwise have been linked. But in many organizations, the narrow view is often rewarded. It's often accompanied by a great focus on a particular task or activity and organizations often reward people for putting in vast amounts of effort in a single field or project. We often reward people in organizations for hav-ing a narrow and single focus. But it is focus taken to an extreme – i.e. overused – forgetting that the connections that haven't happened will never be understood because no one ever saw the possibility of having them.

Being a Narrow Thinker brings major disadvantages, especially if you are trying to introduce new ideas or even just develop the ideas you already have. In many areas of business, a product is very nearly obsolete within a few months of first being put on sale. The really new and even the moderate improvement won't come from just doing more of the same. It will require the ability to link with ideas and data outside of the exist-ing thinking, producing something new by bringing together two existing components that had never been matched before. Once we allow narrow thinking managers to form narrow teams and to operate in narrow organi-zations, vulnerabilities become magnified and the organization is highly susceptible to an imaginative attack from another area.

Consider the oft-told Post-It™ note story. Dr Spencer Silver, working in 3M's central research department, produced a "not very good glue." 3M, being famous for its adhesive, didn't have many supporters for "not

166

very good glue." But Dr Silver recognized that this poor adhesive did not actually strip the surface off paper, so that two pieces of paper could be stuck together and then separated without leaving any kind of a mark. Concurrently, Art Fry, a colleague of Silver's, had a problem. He sang in two different choirs on Sunday and wanted to mark in his hymnbook the different pages for each of the services. His loose paper markings often fell out, so he was delighted to find that by using Silver's adhesive, he could make sticky bookmarks that didn't damage the pages of his hymnbooks. The jump from "not very good glue" via book marks to a new communication system took a lot of persuading. But the product would not have been born if both men had kept within their narrow focus of producing strong adhesives and finding traditional uses for them. Spencer Silver later said, "If I had thought about it, I wouldn't have done the experiment. The literature was full of examples that said you can't do this."

Narrow Thinkers are ...

Narrow Thinkers focus on the here and now and miss possibilities because of their 'tunnel vision' approach.

Signs of Narrow Thinkers

Tell-tale signs

- Described by other people as wearing blinkers.
- Get absorbed in day-to-day activity.
- Have a narrow range of interests and ignore everything else.
- Have very specific reading and viewing interests.

Tell-tale actions

- Focus on a very small number of things.
- Stay within the same field and make links only within that box.
- Make obvious connections, but don't look for the out-of-the-ordinary or the non-obvious.

- Get confused when people bring in other ideas from alternate sources.

- Get deeply absorbed in a single idea or process.

Tell-tale phrases

- "I don't think that's relevant."

- "What has that got to do with it?"

- "I'm not interested in trivia."

- "Please stick to the point and don't wander off the subject."

Case study

The case of the concerned clients

This has been a sad day. I am the senior partner in a small partnership of auditors, trivial in size compared with the larger companies. We have branches in five large towns in the Northwest. Why a sad day? I have just had a call from Michael's final and only client. She told me a story that I've heard many times before in the last two years – that Michael is a lovely man, very attentive, wants to give his clients his best, but he is so narrow. This client said that she wanted to be able to discuss much wider issues than the simple legally required annual audit. She wants to explore business issues, she wants to talk about expansion, she wants a range of consulting skills and she doesn't want to have to go through the same briefing all over again for a new set of consultants. She wants to work with one team and be able to talk to someone she trusts who can offer informal advice as well as formal recommendations to other consulting advice.

Michael has been with the firm for some years now. He joined as a junior and has worked his way up to being a partner in the town where the partnership originally started. Over several years I have noticed that when another office has come up with a new idea, perhaps a new software scheme or a new marketing approach, Michael's office is always the last to take the idea on board. Michael will often steadfastly but politely refuse to use it himself at all, with the result that we have a lop-sided client base. In fact, several of Michael's clients have migrated to partners from other offices. This is not just embarrassing, it's uneconomical because, to retain the client, we have had to offer our services at the same transport cost as providing the local person.

What is it about Michael? Strangely enough, he is not against new technology or new ideas. He was only recently at a partners' meeting arguing, "Of course, we must embrace the new technology," and then a charming pause, "but not me, please." Of course, there was laughter, but there also was cynicism among the up-and-coming partners. They don't see Michael as a role model any more, although his knowledge of his particular aspect of the industry is without question. They see him as a kind of anti-role model. If some of the juniors start to follow his approach of being insistently narrow, we will grow a new range of partners who can't take on the wider and broader business opportunities that we see emerging in some of our go-ahead offices.

I had to speak quite severely with Michael three years ago when we brought in new software. The software adds enormously to our ability to keep costs under control and to offer a tailored service, while taking the tedium out of our audit practice. Michael said that he wanted nothing to do with the process that would turn auditing into a commodity. He didn't agree with the argument that we needed to blend structured software support with our individual intuition and insight.

The loss of Michael's last and only client means that the partners will have to vote on whether he stays as a partner. My guess is that by the weekend he will be facing the challenge of forced retirement. What a pity he couldn't have thought more broadly.

What to do about narrow thinking

1.   The essence of getting broader is to get out of that particular pattern of thought. It may have served you very well, but it also helps you to concentrate on only one area or field of interest. Try this as an exercise. As you are reviewing some kind of problem or question, mentally try to adopt a different perspective. Imagine you are the customer as opposed to the supplier, or try to imagine how your competitor would view the same question. Alternatively, pick on someone in a different industry and ask how they would view the same problem. What you are trying to do is to get a different perspective and therefore a jolt into a different pattern of thought.

2.   "I've never tried it so I know I wouldn't like it." So try something different – music, cinema, or entertainment of some kind. Alternatively, look at a new magazine or a writer you have never read before. Or find out about a department in your organization that you've had no contact with – or a customer.

3.   Narrow people tend to think in the present tense, so deliberately introduce some other tenses into your thinking and your questioning. Ask how your world would have been 100 years ago. Ask how it might be in 20 years. Deliberately pitch back and forth in time to see if you can get a different perspective.

Explore and expand

- Of all the Restrainers this is the one where you are least likely to be aware of the negative effects. Why? Because if you are a Narrow Thinker, you won't look outside your own boundaries to discover your narrowness. So first things first. Look in a feedback mirror. Get some colleagues to give you some feedback about how widely you follow their interests and ideas. Be warned: this may not be a comfortable experience! There's a bullet with your name on it, and you don't know where it's coming from. However, if you stay narrow, you won't last for very long.

- Start easy. You don't have to become a polymath overnight, but begin making ventures into new ground, new territory and new ways of thinking. Also don't abandon the comfort of the thing you are good at. No one said you should abandon your existing skills and passions – merely be aware of what is happening in the rest of the world.

- Start with your own subject area and explore links coming from it. Look for opportunities and reasons to contact other people and other sources of ideas, starting from your own area of expertise. For instance, if you are a lawyer, find connections with something in finance; or if you are an operations person, find connections with human resources.

Note

4.   Brooks, M. (2000) "The border of order," *New Scientist*, January, pp. 37–9.

RESTRAINER 8

TETHERED TO THE PAST

Kodachrome, it gives us those nice bright colors
Gives us the greens of summer
Makes you think all the world's a sunny day, oh, yeah!

Paul Simon, *Kodachrome* (1973)

How good and how old were the 'good old days'?

Being tethered to the past evokes images of grandparent figures sitting on porches, reminiscing about a bygone and sepia-colored past. Nothing so romantic. In the real world at least, the people who live and work their lives based on what worked a generation ago have largely all gone – fired, redundant, retired. The behavior we are shooting for can equally come from the young as well as the older generation. The basic issue stems from security and risk. You have a task to perform, e.g. launch a new product, turn around the efficiency of an emergency room, excavate an archaeological find on a building site. You or your colleagues have done something like this before and you know what worked then. The question is, will what worked then work now? If your instinct is to do again what worked before, you are a **Repeater**. You are tethered to the past. It may be a very recent past, but your assumption is that your world will repeat the conditions you found before.

Of course, you know, because you have had many experiences like this, that because sometimes a situation looks the same as before, things will work out the same. But sometimes they don't. For example, last night you parked illegally and didn't get a ticket; tonight you've parked in the same place and have ended up paying a fine. What happened when you first traveled on an airplane? You followed the safety briefing avidly, whereas now you ignore the briefing and get on with your newspaper, and each time you have ignored the briefing, nothing bad has happened.

Repeaters are often rewarded for delivering a good job because they have used tried and tested approaches that always deliver. They are often more efficient, more reliable, and more successful. But supposing, unknown to anyone, the situation is very slightly different this time? What then?

You are Elmer Perkins, an enormously skilled producer of the highest quality optical equipment. You are producing a mirror 50 times better than any previous mirror, accurate to one millionth of an inch, for the most powerful telescope ever built on earth. Over 16 months, working at night to avoid traffic vibration, which may influence accuracy, you test the mirror to the very limits of the best available technology. It eventually flies in space, as the Hubble Telescope. No one knew that a small piece of paint had chipped from a strut on the mirror test rig, fractionally altering the test standard so that the mirror was ground to very slightly the wrong shape but passed all its final tests. When discovered, a brilliant but costly repair was carried out in space and the Hubble now produces astounding images from further across the universe than has ever been seen before.[5]

"But why did no one build a test of the test rig?" You can hear the siren call of the Repeater here. "It just adds expense. We know what we are doing. It's not needed. It's worked before." And of course, most times Repeaters are right. In this particular case, it was a very high-visibility piece of bad luck. Or *was* it just bad luck?

Repeaters walk a tough tightrope. If they completely flipped their style and wanted to investigate everything from scratch and question everything, hardly anything would get done. On the other hand, never to question and never to wonder if the conditions really are exactly the same this time can lead to disaster. How does the effective manager balance between assuming it will work again this way and questioning everything? We don't believe there is a simple scientific method to answering this question, but we do believe that your instincts may be able to help.

Repeaters are ...

Repeaters are most comfortable repeating past actions because this is the way they have always done it.

Signs of Repeaters

Tell-tale signs

- Seldom look to the future for a way of tackling something.
- Think the world is getting worse.
- Have difficulty accepting criticism of past ideas or methods.
- Do not question the validity of what worked before.
- Believe that age and experience should get more respect than youth and ingenuity.
- Prefer to reminisce rather than to predict.
- Don't want "to boldly go."

Tell-tale actions

- Rate old facts more useful than the most recently discovered ones.
- Remember things as better than they objectively were.
- Speak well of past heroes and ill of new ones.
- Look for guidance from people who have experienced this sort of thing already.

Tell-tale phrases

- "This is the way we've always done it."
- "Don't meddle with what works well enough already."
- "Let's do what worked before."
- "This is the way it worked before. Why should I change?"
- "I think I know how to make this work."
- "We've been here before."
- "I think we should stick to our knitting."

Case study

The case of the resistant repeater

"Dave's one of your most senior people isn't he?" The questioner, who was buying me lunch at a very trendy establishment where the water cost nearly as much as the wine and the beers came from every country except our own, looked concerned. We were on the outskirts of an area known as Silicon Fen (a lowland area of southeast Britain), which now contained more than 12,000 start-up businesses, high-tech businesses, and bioengineering businesses. It was a thriving, exciting place to be. We were both venture capitalists. I was working for a relatively small partnership, but my lunch companion, Jim, was the representative of a major worldwide network – a VC of VC's. His organization had not really developed into the Silicon Fen area yet and my organization had not really moved beyond it. There was potentially a lot of opportunity for both of us.

But Jim kept talking about Dave. "Wasn't Dave one of the original supporters of blahblah.com?" Jim named one of the early successes in dot. com start-ups that had gone on to become a major organization and was now regularly quoted among the top five internet business start-ups. "Yes, he was probably the person who identified the potential of blah before anyone else. I remember at the time we were very unsure about putting money behind what seemed a very tentative proposal. I'm so glad that Dave was able to convince us," I said.

"So what has he done since then?" Jim asked. "Well, he has taken us through a number of organizations," I replied slightly hesitantly. "But have any of them been nearly as successful as blah?" asked my colleague. "Well, no. He hasn't been as lucky since," I replied.

"Tell me the kinds of organizations he's invested in and what his justification has been," he continued. I listed out the other organizations that Dave had invested in or proposed to invest in and an uncanny thing occurred as I was going through the list. I realized that each of the subsequent businesses Dave had proposed putting capital into had some or other kind of link with the now-famous blahblah.com. Under this difficult questioning, I was made to recognize that Dave was a "one-trick pony." Having luckily or insightfully – it doesn't really matter at this distance – fallen into blahblah.com, he then tried to repeat the performance over and over again. Of a dozen or more organizations that he brought to our board meetings, now that I thought about it, each one looked remarkably similar to his original success.

"So what are you saying?" I asked my colleague. "What I'm saying," he said, "is that if we partner with your organization, then I'm sorry, but Dave is going to be on the casualty list. We've looked very carefully at your track record as a VC business in the UK, and to tell you the truth, we are very impressed. You have made a number of very competent investments and you are ahead of the game compared with many in the UK. But Dave is your difficulty. He seems to understand only one kind of company and one kind of situation. In our view, based on what we see in North America, that situation is almost completely gone. The world has moved on several turns and the kind of blahblah start-up Dave so successfully sponsored is not going to happen again in our lifetime."

I was very thoughtful on the drive back from the restaurant. I wanted to take our company into a broader network of other similar organizations. The offer Jim had made was both attractive and offered all of us a far wider range of opportunities to do the kind of work that we loved. But Dave was the problem. If Jim's people were going to work with us, they didn't want to carry Dave. The next company board meeting was going to be a difficult one.

How not to become too tethered to the past

1. Do you really have a limited range of responses to every problem? Or is it that once you've seen something work, you will assume it will work for all time? Draw up a list of as many tasks as you can think of that you tackle as a manager. Now put opposite each task a few words to describe reliable solutions to those tasks. Examine the list and see if you are using the same technique in every case or whether you are using an "it worked once, so it'll work for ever" approach.

2. Having done that, now look for alternative solutions you are prepared to risk on some of those tasks. As with all of these enhancements/suggestions, start with the easy and low-risk first. Then gather up your courage and try something more risky to see what works. How strongly tempted were you to revert to the tried and tested way?

3. For meetings that you run, include in your agenda a request for an alternative way of doing something. Examine your own feelings in asking this question and watch the responses of others. How easy

is it for others to block your attempt to question an existing idea or want to explore a new possibility? You may be a prisoner of your own culture.

4. Try a little time-travel. When relaxing and talking about the good old days, play a little game where the good old days are ones that haven't happened yet. Invent some "good new days" that you'd like to live through. How far can you can brainstorm "looking back on years to come?" Does it give you some ideas? Does it give you confidence to try something slightly different?

Explore and expand

- Because risk is a cultural thing, start exploring what the other cultural clues are in your organization that allow people to take risks, and just as important, that make risk a career-threatening prospect. Look beneath the surface for the really subtle clues that identify the people who are successful supporters of risk in your organization. These are the people whose backing you need if you are attempting to try something different.

- Knowing something worked once often has a subjective component to it. Look around your organization to find examples of what is described as successful, even if sometimes the numbers weren't entirely right. How are people really measuring their success criteria? What are people really ignoring?

Note

5. BBC *Horizon* documentary, written and produced by Jacqueline Smith, BBC, 2000. *See also* the BBC Website: bbc.co.uk/horizon

CHAPTER 5

LEADERSHIP – THE NE(X)T GENERATION

In theory, there is no difference between theory and practice.
But, in practice, there is.

Jan L. A. van de Snepscheut (1993) *What Computing is all About*

In the first part of this book, we've introduced a number of behaviors and skills we believe to be highly relevant to handling unprecedented levels of ambiguity and your own sense of uncertainty. We hope you are using our behavioral suggestions to help you become more effective, more relaxed, and therefore better able to deal with uncertainty.

We have suggested that these might represent another leadership style. When we present our ideas to audiences, we are frequently asked how our ideas fit in with other theories and approaches to leadership. Is there only one "right" way to lead? Are we saying that our approach is right and consequently that others are wrong? Certainly not. We believe that the approach you need to take depends on the context. Effective leadership is finding a good balance between behavior, context and need (*see* Fig. 5.1).

How will more leadership theory help me?

We are going to stand up and fight for theory in this chapter! After all, we all have theories on how our world works. It's what helps us to anticipate and explain what might happen next. As an air traveler, you rely on the safety of the airplane and its systems. You believe that the aerodynamic theory around which all airplanes are designed and built is robust and

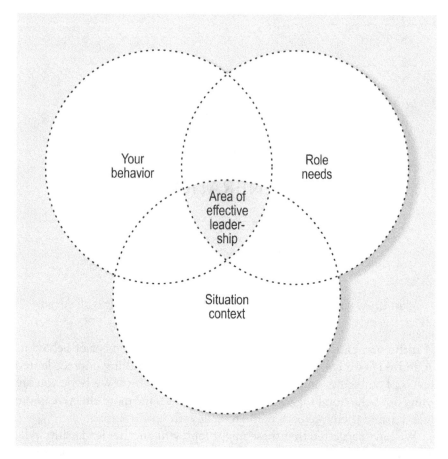

Figure 5.1 ♦ Effective leadership

secure. We've got a surprise for you. Until the mid-1990s the latest understanding of aerodynamic theory only accounted for a small percentage of all take-offs, flights, and landings that occurred every day. Shocked? Well, don't worry because let us quickly remind you that most of the flights each day are those conducted by insects, most of whose wing movements and flight patterns were not explained by standard aerodynamic theory until 1995. So it is OK to fly on airplanes. Fixed-wing aircraft operate within the criteria for prediction, accuracy, quality, and safety that aerodynamic theory has known for nearly 100 years. In 1995 the notion of vortex theory was introduced into aerodynamics to explain the flight of insects.[1] It didn't deny any of the previous work in aerodynamics. Airplanes still fly for the same reasons. However, with vortex theory it became possible to understand the wider range of methods of flight. Soon there will be machines that replicate insect flight, which will create new opportunities to understand *and* develop alternative flying machines.

We believe that even if you have a theory, you must continually chip away at it to see if there's a better way or if it can be made more comprehensive or more thorough. Essentially, that's what we are going to do in this chapter. So let us start with a look at a brief history of leadership.

Take me to your leader

If you view leadership within an historical time frame, then as a leadership researcher, the most useful question you could ask is "Where did the leader come from?" This sounds strange, doesn't it? Surely questions like "What did the leader do?" or "Why did they do it?" would be more helpful. But in ages past, when leaders were rare and unusual beasts, many of them were chosen for leadership roles not because of merit or skill, but because of their background – where they came from. Therefore asking about where they came from told you a lot more than asking questions about their skills, behavior, or personality.

Giovanni Agnelli, the inheritor of the Fiat car fortune, enjoyed in his earlier days a life of the classic international playboy. He was photographed in all the right places with all the right people. Then as a result of a serious car crash in 1952, he reminded himself that his future destiny was to run the Fiat empire. He took over as chairman of Fiat SpA, Italy's largest private business enterprise in 1966. Grandson of Fiat's founder, he said, "I think I took over the chief executive's role a little late in life, but I grew up in this role. I grew up expecting to take over this role."[2]

In 1898 Montague Butler sailed on the SS *Peninsula* to India to take up a senior administrative role as a district officer. The district officers were upper-middle-class public schoolboys. Almost all Oxbridge classicists, they came from the same social class, had been educated together, and in many cases their families were connected.[3]

Gaius Petronius came from a high position in Roman society and belonged to a noble family. He should have won his reputation by effort, but actually he was an idle pleasure-seeker. Even so, he still was appointed to official positions, serving as governor to the Asian province of Bithynia and later becoming the first magistrate of Rome.[4]

The three people above were all born into their jobs. There is little doubt that they attained their role because of family connections and background. They were born into leadership roles – you could almost say that the family business was leadership.

Leaders were born, but now they're grown

Surely all that family and privilege bias is in the past? We select leaders on merit now, don't we? Not completely. There is still a lingering influence from the "leaders are born" era. If you ask leaders of today where they came from, what kinds of answers would you expect? Family would be high on the list. It has been said that a handful of families control a significant percentage of America's wealth.[5] It could be education – the Grande Ecoles in France have produced 90 percent of French leaders in government and business, and in the UK the composition of the British cabinet has been dominated by ministers whose educational background was Oxbridge. It could be geographic location – the Kumasi Kings in Ghana came from that very place. Or it could be a religion – imagine how odd it would have seemed to have had a non-Christian a heartbeat away from the White House (a situation that we were close to in the November 2000 election), or a Catholic heading up the Royal Ulster Constabulary.

So even today, there are some sources that are frequent suppliers of leaders. It would be wrong to think that the assumption that leaders are born is very strong today. There are three main differences in the assumptions from times past compared with today.

1. Today leaders can come from anywhere. In the past they were likely to come from a select group of people.

2. Today everybody feels that they could be a leader, whereas in earlier times most people felt excluded irrespective of their talent, skills, or aptitude.

3. Today defining leadership is a complex matter – and we have much more to say about it in the rest of this chapter. Before, it was simple. Rather in the same way that art is often defined as whatever is done by artists, leadership was defined as whatever was done by people who found themselves in leadership roles. Leadership might have been positive or negative, kind or cruel, but it was whatever the leader did. The notion of leadership development was almost an oxymoron.

All of these are examples where leadership and influence came naturally and without question and, if we're being tough about this, without any kind of evaluation.

The inherited leader may fit the behavior and context really well. But because their qualification for being in the role is their background, there's a likelihood that they may not be good at managing change. The inherited leader may be rooted in the past and clinging to previous aims and methods. Additionally, their prime linkage to their followers is frequently to demand compliance, not because of what the leader does, but because of who the leader is. In short, the leader is born to lead and the followers are born to follow.

War Office WOSBIES

It is arguable whether there was ever a single moment in history when there was a dramatic shift from choosing leaders because of their background to choosing leaders because of their skills. Certainly there is a case for claiming that the Industrial Revolution in Europe was a time when a lot of people who did not have the "right" background were still able to make their mark on the world. They created their fortunes and then used the power of that money to install themselves in leadership roles. These were leaders who were made not born. However, we would choose the period of the Second World War as one of the most significant turning points in the progression of leadership understanding and leadership development. Prior to that time there was very little research or structured work done on selecting leaders for their skills and competencies. However, during the Second World War a need arose that required competing organizations to rapidly identify and understand what effective leaders did and then work out how to select them.

The military forces of the Axis and Allied powers were all running out of commanders faster than they could be recruited from the traditional sources. Each side had to tackle the same problem. Where do we find new people who can be commanders who don't come from the traditional backgrounds?

Each organization approached the problem in a remarkably similar way, although at the time it appears that even the Allies didn't mention it to each other. They all developed various versions of what we now would call the "assessment center." They analyzed as best they could what were the activities, behaviors, and attributes necessary to be an effective commander in the military forces. They then sought ways of identifying people who had those skills or that particular potential. Assessment techniques like the paper-and-pencil test, the psychological inventory, the physical problem-solving exercise, the structured interview, and so on were all developed around this time. The War Office Selection Board (WOSB) in the UK and the Office of Strategic Services (OSS) in the US were the first emergent examples of the assessment center. This technology now has a major influence over many countries and many organizations.[6]

The task and the people

After the Second World War, the researchers who had worked in Germany, the US, and Britain went into industry or back into university psychology departments. What emerged after a number of years were some now classically quoted cases, such as Westinghouse. Scientists reported that the behavior of leaders could be categorized on a map (*see* Fig. 5.2).

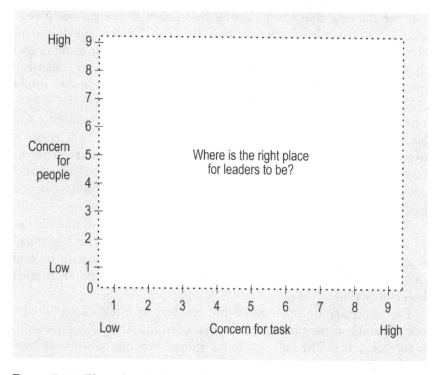

Figure 5.2 ♦ The task and the people

The leader's behavior was composed of two main aspects: concern for the task and concern for the people who did the task.

There followed a series of debates which lasted ten or more years about where the effective leader should be on the chart. Should they be over-concerned with the task and not about the people? Should they be over-concerned with the people and not with the task? Should they try to do both, and was that possible? What happened to the people who scored 0, 0? Were they clinically dead?!

A variety of solutions to this problem emerged, where it was identified that the situation the leader was trying to handle was the key influencer in the style and behavior that the leader should adopt. How then to identify the situation?

Situational solutions

One very popular method called situational leadership (drawn from what became known as The Ohio State Studies) described the development of the follower.[7] It is widely known and a very useful approach to describing some leadership skills. The follower who knew very little on entry into the organization would need clear structure and instructions to do a good job. The leader would take full responsibility for the task and would need to give clear instruction to the follower, so that the follower could achieve useful output. You will no doubt be familiar with figures like Fig. 5.3. The follower develops their knowledge skills and their understanding of the tasks needed so the leader can shift the style that he or she uses towards the follower. In Fig. 5.3 four options are given.

Command and control

This is command and control leadership. The effective leader can super-vise his or her followers because they know at least as much about the task as the follower does. They are able to choose an appropriate behav-ioral style depending on their judgment of the level of knowledge and motivation and understanding that the follower has for the task. This is a kind of leadership through expertise. Because the leader knows a lot about the tasks, he or she can structure, coach, support, or delegate to followers appropriately. It has to be said that many managers, while being aware of the need to change their style according to the follow-ers' needs, actually have a strong preference for a particular style. They

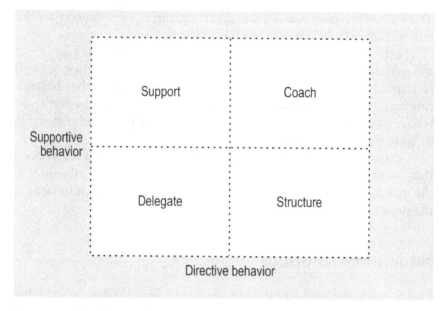

Figure 5.3 ◆ Leadership and the situation command and control
Source: Adopted form Blanchard *Situational Leadership* (1994)

therefore often tend to use one style inappropriately. This can lead to all kinds of problems and issues as followers receive too much or too little structure.

In organizations where the command and control style is the prevalent leadership type, promotion is usually based on technical competence. Nonetheless, it is a very effective way of thinking about leadership when known tasks are being done by people who know how to do them.

Currently, many consulting firms and partnerships employing specialists like auditors, tax experts, architects, or lawyers use this type of leadership quite widely because it is an information-based approach. The senior partner knows more than the junior and therefore applies their knowledge to guide the junior to do their best work. At the time when these ideas were being first discussed (in the 1970s), there was little distinction made between management and leadership. The words were for most purposes interchangeable. Now we notice that many people describe this type of leadership behavior as management.

I have a dream ...

What do you do if you don't know how to achieve your goal? What happens if, like Dr Martin Luther King Jr, you want to achieve a dream? You want to move towards a point which, although desirable for many, is breathtakingly far away for most. No one knew what steps were needed to actually achieve that goal in practice. How do you promise, as John F. Kennedy did in a speech to Congress on May 25 1961, "Before this decade is out [we will] land a man on the moon and return him safely to the earth," when at the time the rocket technology that was available was way below the standard and power needed to achieve that aim? How do you take a run-down and loss-making national transport company as Colin Marshall did with British Airways in the 1970s and '80s and turn it into what some described as "the world's favorite airline"?

You empower people to achieve your vision. But as many organizations found in the romantic 1980s and early '90s, having a vision and peppering your conversations with the 'V' word wasn't good enough. Frankly, anyone can have a vision. Drink a bottle of liquor and in 20 minutes you'll have visions (please don't try this too often!), but they may not be of any practical business value to you. Visions don't work unless the people who have to find their way to the vision are given sufficient empowerment to take the actions necessary to reach the vision without continually needing to refer back to their leader.

Compared with command and control leadership, empowering leadership was designed for a different context, offered different kinds of outcomes and required very different behavior. People who had grown up with command and control leadership continued to expect predictability, accuracy, and the dominance of knowledge and experience. They were frequently going to be disappointed.

The true visionary leader allows the followers to be highly empowered so they have the flexibility to take whatever actions are necessary to achieve the vision. Many leaders from the previous era were unwilling in practice to give up their own power by empowering others.

Hence, we arrive in our own time era. The two main forms of leadership that have been used and understood in organizations are:

1.   the command and control approach, where leaders are controllers and experts

2.   the empowerment and visionary approach, where leaders are visionaries and empowerers.

Sadly, when we look around many organizations, what we often find is empowerment words and control actions. This results in the worst of both worlds. We want people to be imaginative, risk-taking, and creative, but still to return their projects on time, on budget and be able to forecast the outcome of the next quarter to the nearest dollar. We want organizations to learn more clearly to recognize which of these two leadership styles is more appropriate to which context. Both are fine in the right context but will work very badly in the wrong context. Unfortunately, there is an emotional difficulty to be overcome. For the most part, people find the notion of being visionary leaders more romantic and attractive than being controlling managers. Hence, the command and control approach tends to have a poorer image than that of the empowering and visionary leader. But both methods work well in their own contexts. The question that modern leaders have to ask themselves on a daily – if not hourly – basis is, "What is the right method for this particular context?"

> ... when we look around many organizations, what we often find is empowerment words and control actions.

A new leadership style – learning leadership

Learning is what most adults will do for a living in the 21st century.

S. J. Perelman (1904–79)

So what do you do if you don't have a vision? After Lou Gerstner took over IBM on April Fool's Day in 1993, one of his first public statements was, "The last thing IBM needs now is a vision."[8] He knew that the company had a huge amount of talent within it, but he didn't really know what the talent was capable of or what opportunities there really were. What happens if you aren't ready for vision yet? What happens if, like Jeff Bezos (the creator of Amazon.com), you really don't know what could be sold on the internet or whether people would really trust this virtual system of selling. Could you have a clear vision of the future? What happens if you are a venture capitalist and someone comes to you with a 500-word proposal that seems so hot that you don't even feel it is worth waiting for the time and trouble of a proper business plan to be put together?

As in each of these cases, people in leadership roles are faced with huge levels of inherent ambiguity in their situation. They are uncertain, and of course, that is probably rather stressful. However, in all of these cases, what the participants did was move toward the uncertainty, not away from it. If there really is a third style of leadership emerging – that of learning leadership – its defining feature will be leaders noted for their tendency to head *toward* uncertainty and ambiguity. To survive in a tough, ambiguous environment, difficult learning is the key (*see* p. 45).

> If there really is a third style of leadership emerging – that of learning leadership – its defining feature will be leaders noted for their tendency to head *towards* uncertainty and ambiguity.

Why don't we include visionary leadership with ambiguity leadership? We would argue that in visionary leadership the leader is normally quite clear and quite certain about what the vision should be. Of course, there is still much uncertainty in interpreting the vision of the leader, but this now becomes a communication issue, not a direction issue. The visionary leader says to the followers, "Let's work together on how to make my vision happen." Whereas, the leader in ambiguity says, "Let's work together on how we can learn what the vision should be."

In our 1996 book, *The Future of Leadership*, we defined the leader's role as:

Identifying productive areas of uncertainty and confusion and leading the organization into those areas to gain competitive or other kinds of advantage.

This is the situation that we have observed many of today's executives finding themselves in – whether they like it or not. Many of their instincts will be to avoid ambiguity and uncertainty and to install certainty by making clear and firm statements. The problem is that today's organizational world is in such a volatile state that it is much harder now than it was 20 years ago to make such clear and firm statements accurately.

The pressures on this new kind of leader will be immense. First, to what extent can they really admit to their followers that they don't know? In early 1999, Reuters chief executive Peter Job said at an analysts and journalists briefing, "... it is hard to be clear about the strategy at the moment" and in one day $1.2 billion was wiped off the company's share price.[9] Later, on February 8, 2000, when Mr Job unveiled Reuter's long-awaited internet strategy, he was greeted by a round of applause from the analysts and the company's stock rose by 20 percent. The difficult question here is how much can a CEO tell the truth when the truth is that you don't yet know? In Peter Job's case, it seems, he and his company were punished severely for telling the truth.

An equally tough requirement for learning leaders is to recognize that learning from their mistakes needs to be at least as public as learning from their successes. Everyone in the organization has to engage in continuous learning, and some of that learning may challenge existing concepts and require genuinely original solutions. Here the leader's job is again to take the organization toward things it doesn't know, in search of fruitful new ideas and original learning. This may account for the spate of truth-telling (almost confessional) CEO's – from United Airlines to Ford Motor Company – appearing on US television in the summer of 2000, each apologizing to the American consumer and asking for patience as the organization learns to correct a major problem.[10]

Look at Fig. 5.4. If you are a learning leader, then you are going to want to spend most of your own and your organization's time in the top right-hand quadrant doing things that are difficult to learn, but which are of high value to the organization. A colleague described it as the "*Star Trek* strategy;" that is, you boldly go where no one has gone before! Certainly, the only thing that guarantees your success if you want to spend a lot of your organization's time in that arena is the quality of learning that your organization can muster. Because you don't know how to do the things that you will come across in that quadrant, you must be able to learn very rapidly under the toughest of conditions to survive and prosper. It is certainly not for everyone. But people who do operate at this level will describe it as thrilling, exciting, and challenging.

David Grossman and John Patrick of IBM won over CEO Lou Gerstner in an instant. "Where's the buy button?" he is reputed to have asked.[11] But they still had to spend a lot of effort to bring the IBM of 1994–5 to the realization that the internet could mean big and strategically significant business for the recovering company. John Patrick was continually asked how IBM could make money from the new internet and candidly admitted that he had no idea. Nonetheless, he was clear that the internet would become the most powerful and important form of communication both inside and outside the corporation.

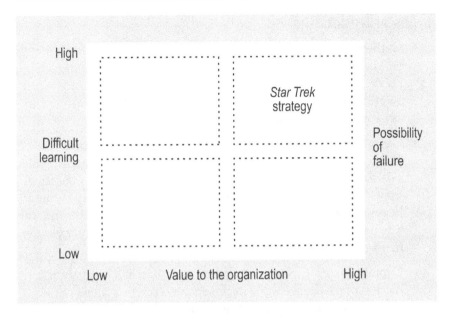

Figure 5.4 ♦ Difficult learning and competitive advantage
Source: Adapted from *The Future of Leadership* 1996

Do you want to test how much your organization is using the third model of leadership? Ask your people to name five important products, services, and production techniques now taken for granted, but which a previous generation of managers would not have known. Now list five trends in products, services, and production techniques the next generation will take for granted, but which you can hardly fathom. The pathway to installing those trends so that they become real is the amount of difficult learning facing you and your colleagues. If it is substantial, then develop your difficult learning skills or get out of the business.

Beam me up, Scotty

When our colleague – a committed "Trekkie" – suggested the "*Star Trek* strategy" as a useful title for the quadrant on the difficult learning map (*see* Fig. 5.4), he wondered aloud if we couldn't also characterize the different leadership types we had identified. If you are allergic to *Star Trek*, please feel free to skip this part.

Types of leadership

- **Catherine Janeway – learning leader.** Her characteristic phrase is "Let's give it a try." She's clearly encouraging learning in all her crew. She doesn't know how to do it, but she is prepared to have a go at it, using the strength of her crew and herself to learn how to cope with the problem.

- **Captain Jean-Luc Picard – empowering leader.** His phrase is "Make it so." He usually gets his group around him in a crisis and asks for suggestions, but then he makes the decision and has them implement it. He would be largely an empowering leader because he empowers his people to make suggestions, but he is the one who sets the overall vision and overall goal. They have to carry out the management necessary to achieve that goal.

- **Captain James T. Kirk – command and control.** Strangely, the hardest of the leadership styles to characterize in a single phrase is the plan, organize, and control style. Trekkies that we know say instinctively that it is the "Captain Kirk style." He leads, he commands, he knows. In a crunch he is better than any of his crew with any of the technologies, but he doesn't seem to have a characteristic phrase. So if he is true to the type we have allocated to him, he would say something like, "Do it as I say."

Toward a comprehensive leadership map

We have identified three possible leadership types, each appropriate for a different context. We dispute the widely held view that there is one kind of leadership, one set of behaviors, or one set of skills that will work in all situations. Our hope is that the reader will be able to identify the several contexts in which they lead and to choose the appropriate type of leadership to fit that context.

Do leaders manage or do managers lead?

As you may recall from what we said in Chapters 1 and 2, we are more interested in identifying useful behaviors than arguing taxonomies of leadership and management. We do, however, recognize that in many organizations distinctions are made between leadership and management that have relevance and meaning in diverse areas ranging through status and pay to training and development needs.

So how would we define the difference between leadership and management? We think there are three parts to this question.

1. **Context one – I know what to do and how to do it.** If you know what you want to do and you know how to do it, you are likely to be using a **command and control** type of leadership. You value your expertise and ability to predict accurately what will happen next. In this context, leaders tend to be defined as the people with the most responsibility (command) and the most power (or the greatest ability to control). People who follow the controls and commands of others tend to be called managers.

2. **Context two – I know what to do but not how to do it.** If you are in a situation where you know what you want to achieve, but you don't know how to get there, then you are likely to be using an **empowerment** type of leadership. In this context, the leader is the person with the vision and who gives away significant parts of their own power and responsibility to empowered managers who have to work out *how* to reach the vision or goal. Taking on the role of leader without the readiness to empower and taking on the role of manager without the necessary empowerment are both tantamount to a death wish!

3. **Context three – I don't know what to do or how to do it.** We believe that a third situation is emerging, where you know neither what you can achieve nor how to get there. The overriding necessity for you and your organization is to be able to learn, grow and change faster than the competition. In other words, your survival depends on your ability to learn. In this context the leader is likely to be the person who has the greatest tolerance for risk and the greatest preparedness to head toward organizational and personal uncertainty. The managers in this context are the people who are the **learner followers** who share in the risk and the learning. Their role will be to minimize risk when possible, but to take risks when necessary. The leader will move toward the greatest level of uncertainty to offer the opportunity to gain the greatest opportunity from that uncertainty.

Overall, we see no absolute difference between leadership and management that applies in every case to every organization in every historic age. It really does depend on the context.

The leaders of today and tomorrow are both free and constrained at the same time. They are free to choose from a wider range of strategies and opportunities than has arguably ever existed before, but at the same time, they are constrained as leaders to be responsible for the potential of the new and undiscovered. Their uncertainty skills will be tested "to the max" if they are to be responsible for a continually coherent, improving, and relaxing world rather than a continually dysfunctional, unraveling, and stressful world.

Notes

1. Brooks, M. (1997) "On a wing and a vortex," *New Scientist*, October 11. Also Hall, A. (1999) "Fly like a fly," *Scientific American*, June 21 and Scott, P (1999) "A bug's life," in *Scientific American*, April.

2. *The Money Makers: Italy's Uncrowned King* (1986) BBC film.

3. BBC History Zone film (2000) *The Last Years of the Raj*, written and directed by Caterine Clay. Visit the BBC Website: bbc.co.uk/history

4. Gaius Petronius (*see* britannica.com)

5. Domhoff, G.W. (1998) *Who Rules America?* Mayfield Publishing Company. *See also* Mills, C.W. (1956) *The Power Elite*. Oxford, England: Oxford University Press, Galaxy Books.

6. Stewart, V. and Stewart, A. (1977) *Tomorrow's Men Today*. London: Institute of Personnel Management.

7. Hersey, R (1984) *The Situational Leader*. Escondido, CA: Center for Leadership Studies. See also Blanchard, K. (1994) "Situational leadership, the article." Blanchard Training & Development, Inc.

8. Morris, B. (1997) "He's smart. He's not nice. He's saving Big Blue," *Fortune*, April 14.

9. "Job's patience may not save Reuters," *The Times*, October 22,1999, p. 35.

10. Taylor, A. (2000) "Jac Nasser's biggest test," *Fortune*, September 18, p. 123.

11. Hamel, G. (2000) "Waking up IBM: how a gang of unlikely rebels transformed Big Blue," *Harvard Business Review*, July-August, pp. 137–46.

CHAPTER 6

FIELD NOTES FROM THE FRONTLINE

---

*Leaders of tomorrow are the ones who today think
about the next big ideas.*

Percy Barnvik

I f you've made it this far, congratulations! These are our field notes, and
during this book we've been inviting you to read them over our shoul-
der. We've taken an anthropological point of view to study what we'd
most like to help you be: an effective leader of a successful organization.
Our struggle in the rendering of these field notes has been how to capture
the essence of leadership *in vivo*. We've thrown away others' viewpoints
and their categorizations of what leaders do – we feel they lead us into
documenting sameness and missing the changes/struggles that our clients
and those in our classrooms are grappling with.

Everywhere we go there is excitement and dread – the excitement of
change and the dread of coping. People want to lead well and people want
to follow well. The trouble is that they don't know how; there are no real
instruction manuals. The manuals available presuppose a world we hardly
encounter – a world where all the critical variables are accounted for
and all the relevant information is known or assumed away. It is a world
where "all things being equal ...," "rational man" exists, using straight-line
extrapolations into the future.

So, as crazy as it is (or as crazy as we sound), this has been our attempt
to document the skills and perspectives we see as critical for success/
effectiveness as a leader or follower. With due respect to Kelley's work
on followership: to lead you must be able to follow.[1] Everybody follows

something or someone, and of course, in a matrixed environment, you might lead the project team in the morning and I might lead in the afternoon.

Not everyone reading this book is or wants to be a leader. These are choices each of us has to make, but in some way each of us is responsible for developing leadership. It may be with our children, with the high-potential who works with you on a project, with your niece coming for career advice, or it may be your spouse struggling to understand their impact on a project team. Each of these is an occasion where understanding the behavior of effective leaders is important, potentially helpful, and hopefully beneficial.

Building on the French social historian DeTocqueville's 200-year-old observations on democracy in America, we all have a stake in developing leaders. It's a societal requirement. Furthermore, these requirements are being raised, they are higher. It is no longer enough for leaders to simply know the most, come from the right families, or be the ones with the vision. Today's leaders must be comfortable in an age of uncertainty, because leadership is a problem and an opportunity everyone has to deal with. You never know when or where the next brilliant idea will come from ...

Is that it?

Sir Bob Geldof [2]

This is not the end. It is not even the beginning of the end. But it is, perhaps, the end of the beginning.

Winston Churchill [3]

What's the Big Idea?

The Tick [4]

Suppose you are sitting at your desk going about your normal everyday business when suddenly you are struck by a brilliant new idea, one that will transform your market or your work. What do you do? How do you cope? Carl Jung, the Swiss psychologist, taught us that new ideas frequently happen simultaneously around the world – he called it synchronicity.[5] It is likely that for every occasion that the same idea hits several minds and gets picked up and used (i.e. calculus being invented by Leibnitz and

Newton; evolution being proposed by Darwin and Wallace; and the periodic table by Mendeleev, Newlands, and Meyer), there must be many more times when ideas hit and no one picks them up. Why is that?

The uncertainty of the new

A big idea carries with it a big responsibility. If understood and developed, nothing will be quite the same again. Once Grossman and Patrick had been struck by the significance of the internet and pushed and pulled to get IBM to become internet-aware, neither their lives nor the IBM culture would ever be the same again (*see* Chapter 5). Once Galileo Galilei had been struck by the significance of Copernicus's tentative and largely posthumously published conclusions, he was on a collision course with the authorities of the day (*see* Chapter 3). Uncertainty had been unleashed and neither Galileo nor the Church would ever be the same again. Yet it took the Church until 1992 to officially recognize Galileo's radical conclusion as correct – 360 years of official ambiguity and uncertainty in the face of one man's big idea. No doubt there are some IBM staffers tucked away in a corner somewhere who, more than a decade after Grossman and Patrick started their revolution, still are uncertain that this is the right way to go.

The responsibility of the new

The best-selling fantasy and comedy writer Terry Pratchett suggests the existence of particles of raw inspiration.[6] Like subatomic particles, they fly through the universe all the time randomly colliding with other matter, each releasing a burst of creativity before being destroyed. If the matter they collide with is a brick or a frog, not much happens. But just occasionally a particle collides with a receptive mind and becomes a new idea.

Just suppose Pratchett is right and our minds are constantly being bombarded with new idea particles releasing little bursts of creativity. What happens next? A new idea brings with it uncertainty of how to use that idea, who will approve, who will disapprove? What kind of a world does this lead to if we are unable to cope with the consequences and responsibilities of the new? What kinds of societies, organizations, or leaders would we expect? Some would say that it leads to a world pretty much like our own world or at least until very recently, a "Dilbert world," where new ideas are for the most part frowned upon and shunned. People having new ideas or displaying creative curiosity are called derogatory names like "nerds," "eggheads," and "mad inventors."

People with great ideas, like Sir Frank Whittle, the inventor of the jet engine, or Sir Christopher Cockerell, the inventor of the hovercraft, are stalled by governments and sometimes society in general. Cockerell's father said his son (who registered more than 70 patents) was "no more than a garage hand." Often the world prefers to listen to grand people like Lord Kelvin saying in 1900, "There is nothing new to be discovered in physics now. All that remains is more and more precise measurement." Or maybe they find Niccolo Machiavelli more comforting, saying 500 years ago, "There is nothing more difficult to take in hand, more perilous to conduct, or more uncertain in its success, than to take the lead in the introduction of a new order of things."[7]

> ... expertise means an ability to learn by doing things different and doing different things each time.

Imagine instead a world where most people have developed the skills to embrace ambiguity and uncertainty and thus have real confidence to encourage the new and original. When the new idea particle collides with these minds, the responsibility of the new is welcomed, explored, and realized. What kind of world would it be where new ideas are not greeted with choruses of "it won't work," "it's been done before," "there's no use for that," and recognized expertise is not based on doing the same thing over and over again? It might be a world where the response to a new idea is more akin to "that's interesting," "how can we develop that?" or "how can we make better use of it?" And expertise means an ability to learn by doing things different and doing different things each time. A world where "I don't know" is not taken as an admission of failure, but actually means, "I don't know, but I want to find out."

Have we evolved far enough to cope with such a world? We don't know, but we'd certainly invite you to help us find out. We think it might encourage us all to become more r e l a x e d.

Notes

1.   Kelley, R. (1992) *The Power of Followership: How to Create Leaders People Want to Follow and Followers Who Lead Themselves*. New York: Doubleday Books.

2. Geldof, B. (1987) *Is That It?* London: Weidenfeld and Nicholson.

3. Churchill, W. L. S. (1942) Speech at the Lord Mayor's Luncheon, Mansion House, November 10, London.

4. Cartoon Superhero, circa 1994.

5. Jung, C. G. (1973) *Synchronicity*. Translated by R. F. Hill. Princeton, NJ: Princeton University Press.

6. Pratchett, T. (1989) *Wyrd Sisters*, p. 59. London: Corgi.

7. Niccolò Machiavelli (1469–1527), Italian political philosopher and statesman. His most famous writing, *The Prince* (1532), describes the means by which a leader may gain and maintain power. His "ideal" prince was an amoral and calculating tyrant; hence, the term "Machiavellian."

CPSIA information can be obtained
at www.ICGtesting.com
Printed in the USA
BVHW042349190221
600627BV00013B/569

9 780578 713533